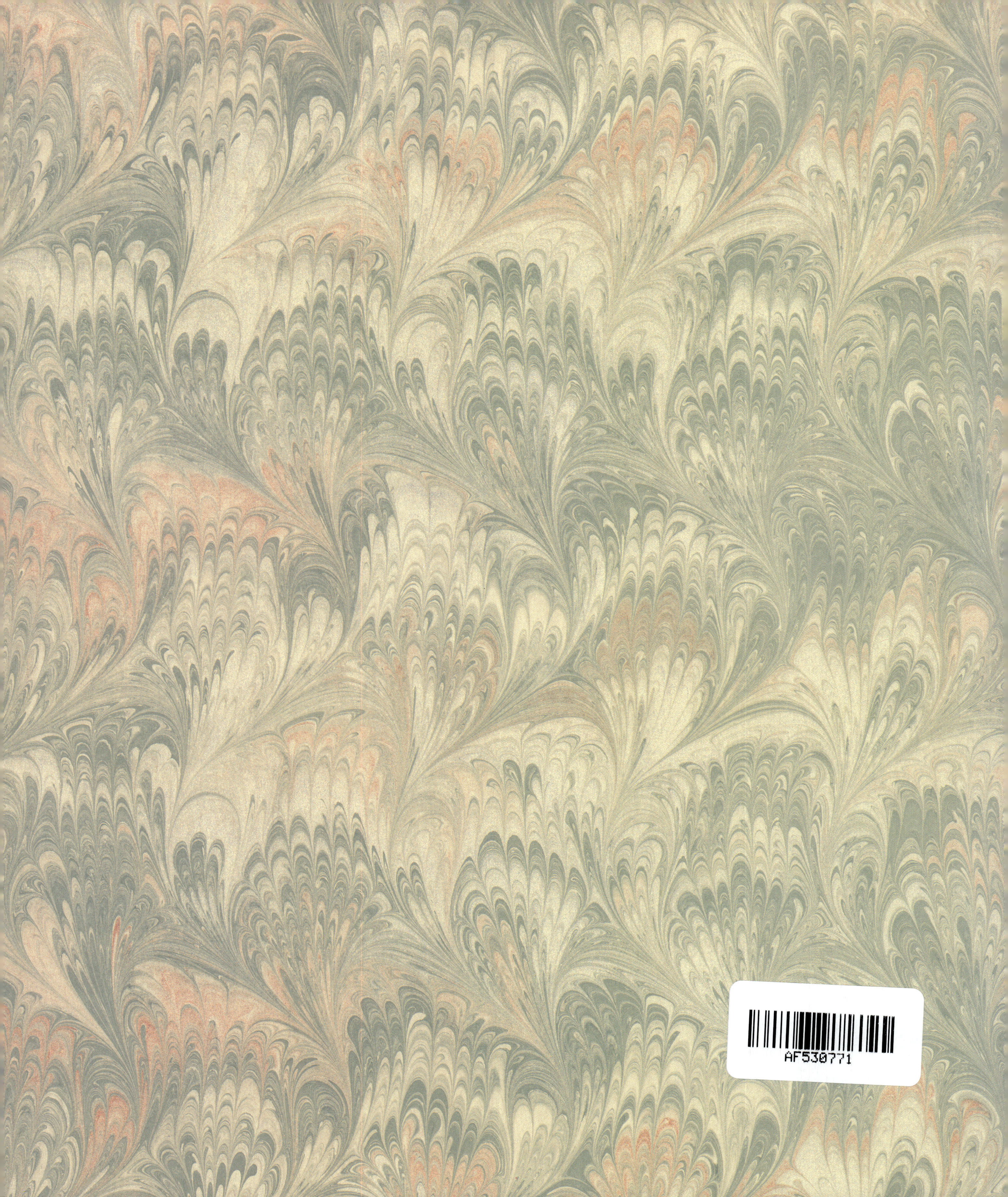

CELEBRATIONS IN ART

A PASSION FOR FLOWERS

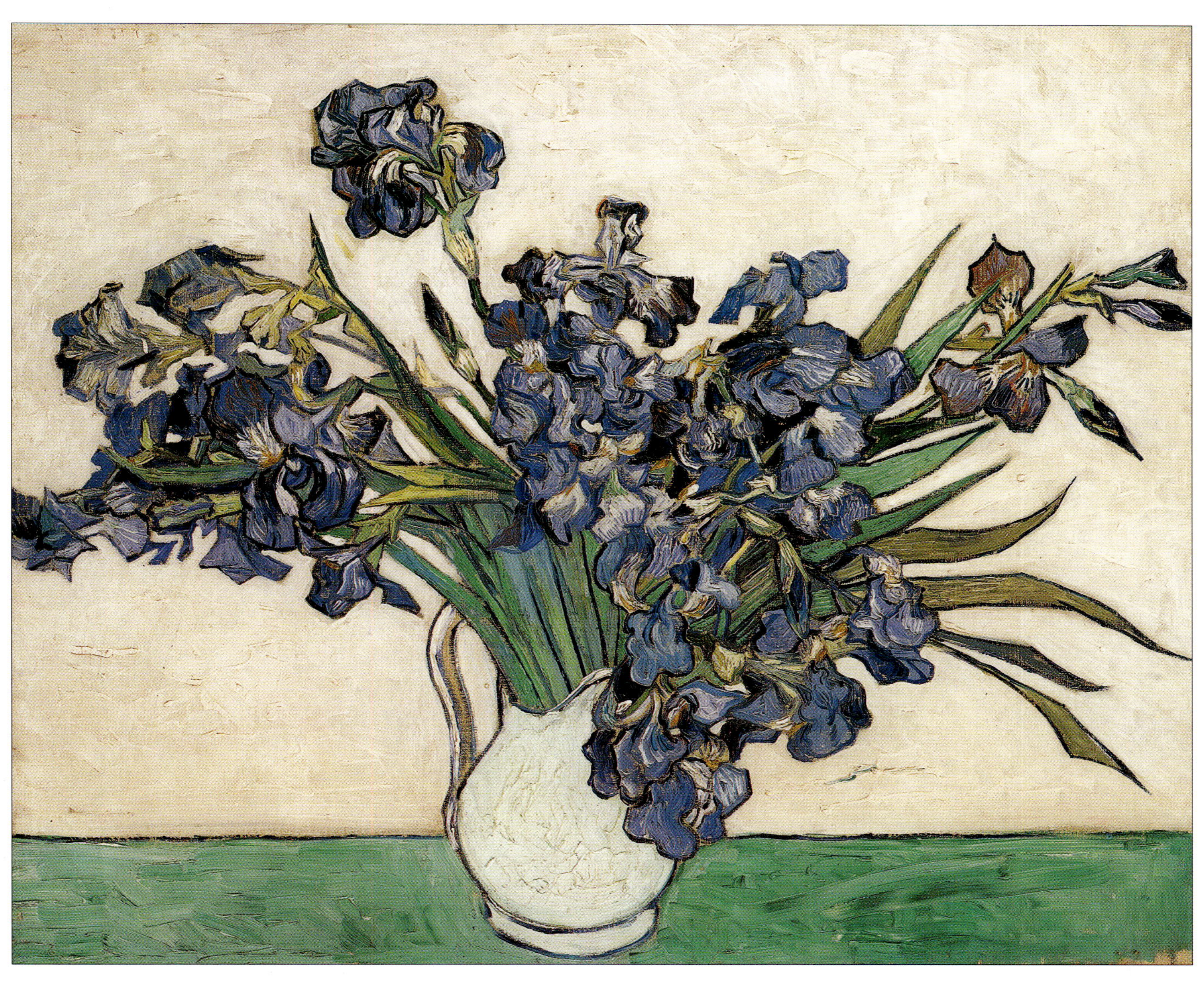

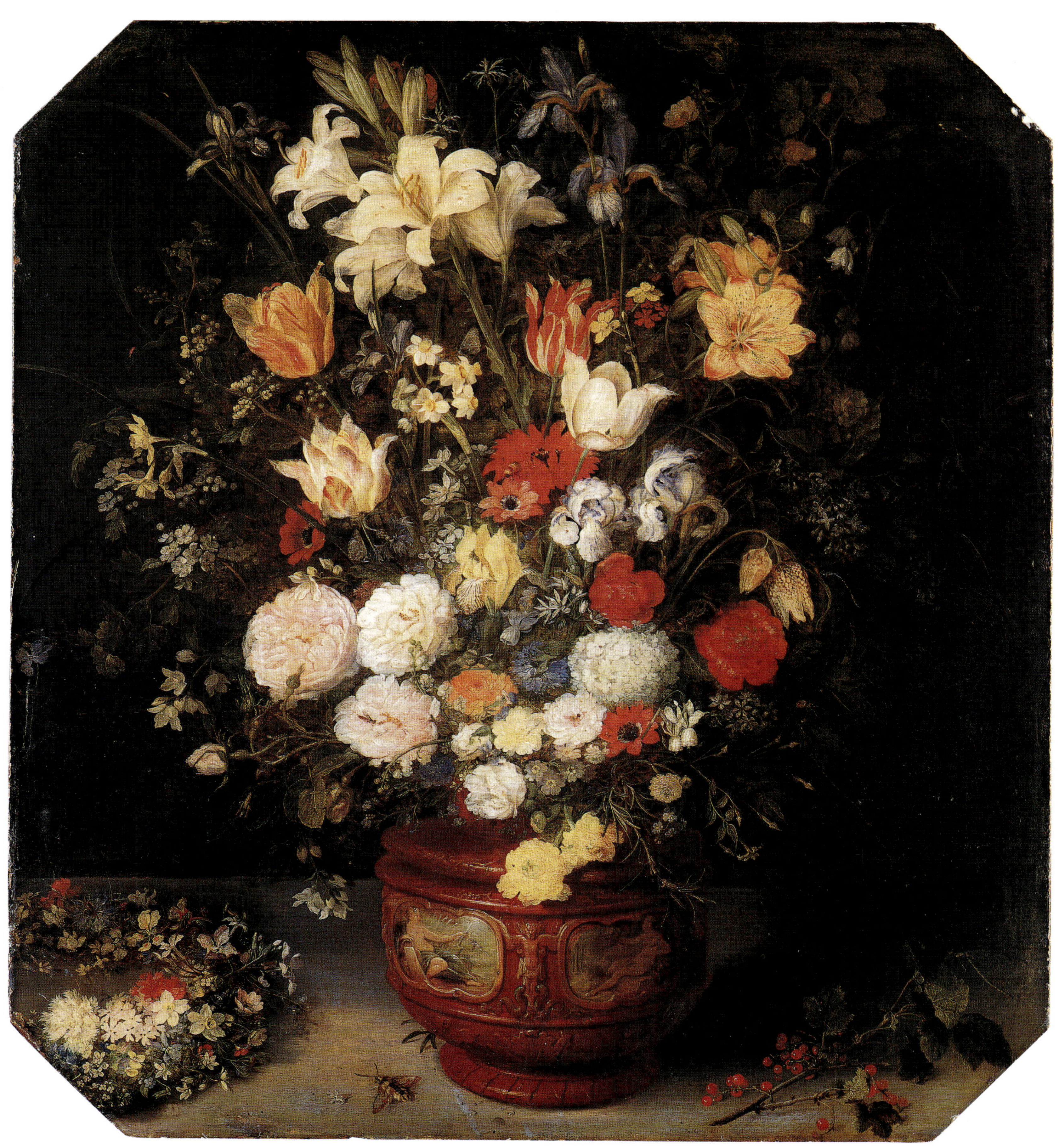

Celebrations in Art

A Passion for Flowers

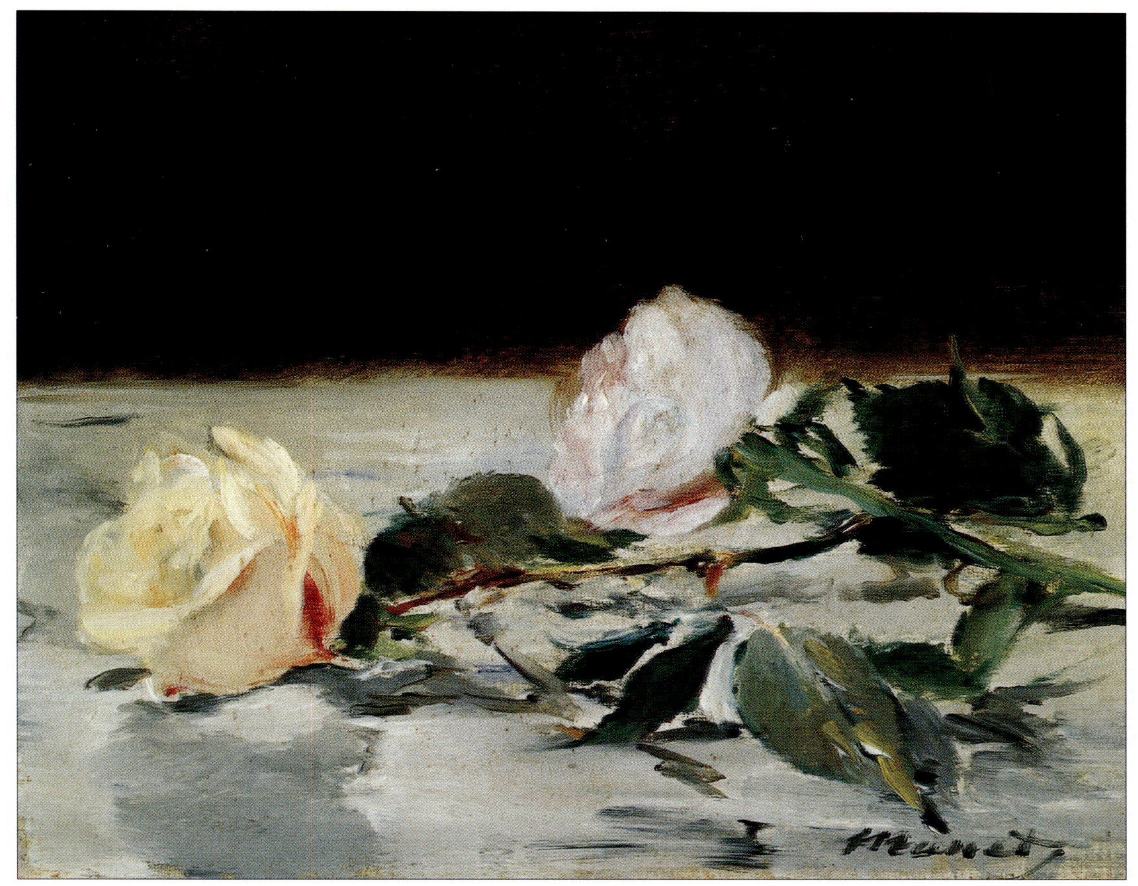

ALEXANDRA BONFANTE-WARREN

MetroBooks

MetroBooks
AN IMPRINT OF FRIEDMAN/FAIRFAX PUBLISHERS

Library of Congress Cataloging-in-Publication Data available upon request

ISBN 1-56799-294-3

Editor: Sharyn Rosart
Production Editor: Loretta Mowat
Art Director: Jeff Batzli
Designers: Lynne Yeamans and Lori Thorn
Photography Editor: Wendy Missan
Production Coordinator: Marnie Ann Boardman

Color separations by HK Scanner Arts Int'l Ltd.
Printed in China by Leefung-Asco Printers Ltd.

For bulk purchases and special sales, please contact:
Friedman/Fairfax Publishers
Attention: Sales Department
15 West 26th Street
New York, NY 10010
212/685-6610 FAX 212/685-1307

Additional Photography Credits: Page 1: Vincent van Gogh, *Irises*, 1890. Oil on canvas, 29" × 36¼" (73.7 × 93.1cm). The Metropolitan Museum of Art, New York City. Page 2: Jan Brueghel the Elder, *Bouquet of Flowers*, c. 1619–1620. Oil on oak panel, 25¼" × 23¼" (64.1 × 59cm). Preussiches Kulturbesitz, Nationalgalerie, Staatliche Museen zu Berlin. Page 3: Édouard Manet, *Two Roses on a Tablecloth*, 1882–1883. Oil on canvas, 7⅝" × 9½" (19.3 × 24.2cm). The Museum of Modern Art, New York City. Page 5: Henri Fantin-Latour, *Bouquet of Roses and Nasturtiums in a Vase*, 1883. Oil on canvas, 11" × 14" (28 × 36cm). The Hermitage, Saint Petersburg.

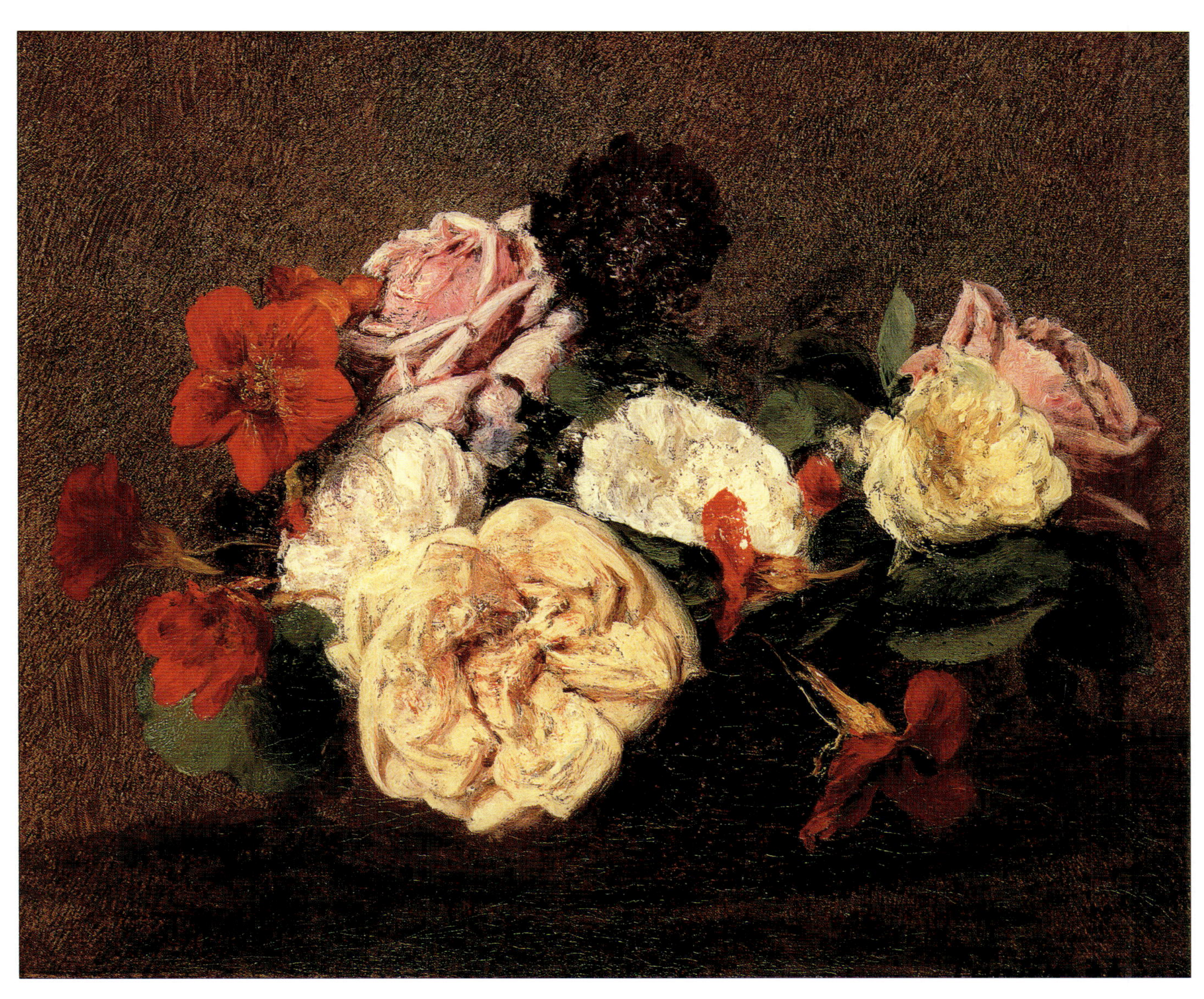

For Vittoria Dompé Bonfante

Introduction

> To see a world in a grain of sand
> And a heaven in a wild flower…
> —William Blake

Around the globe, people have long treasured flowers—for their healing powers (and occasionally for their harmful qualities), as symbols of the melancholy and splendid transience of life, or simply for their own incomparable beauty.

The ancient Italians even worshiped a goddess of flowers: Flora. Religions of all types celebrate the arrival of spring and its blooms, whether with Passover, Easter, or other festivals. We greet the end of winter with exhilaration. Small children stoically accept the autumn passing of flowers, unaware that buds will burgeon again. (Even as adults, some of us are secretly relieved each time spring has sprung once more.) If we allow ourselves, we will be awed by the extravagant beauty of blossoms and their implicit promises of bountiful autumn harvests to come.

Flowers are both various and alike, their shapes and colors always delightful to the eye. Flowers cheer us up, express our rejoicing or mourning; we bring them to court our beloved, to apologize, to celebrate, to treat our eyes.

In most times and places around the world, flowers, the harbingers of spring, have made their way into art, often transformed into abstract and therefore enduring symbols. The tapestries of medieval France, the carpets of Timurid Persia, the fabrics of China, the screens of Japan, the wallpapers of William Morris—these and more are manifestations of the desire to bring the outside in, to surround ourselves with the singular splendor of flowers.

What is it that fascinates us in these gifts of nature? They are sometimes simple, sometimes bafflingly complex, lavished by a prodigal providence upon the earth. Far from diminishing their appeal, the ordinary fact that their splendor, variety, and profusion serve the practical purpose of perpetuating themselves makes them all the more miraculous.

The freshness of Blake's insight reminds us that we still, as much as our neighbors and forebears of every time and place, see in the world around us the reflections of other worlds. From a three-thousand-year-old Egyptian funerary papyrus (c. 1039–991 B.C.) to the acrylic brilliance of David Hockney's *Mount Fuji and Flowers* (1972) to Mary Frank's eccentric untitled amaryllis (1977), flowers have reflected cultural and private associations alike. The elect who unrolled the Theban scroll read the hieroglyphics, but they also read the image of the lotus—a symbol of rebirth, like the god Osiris to whom the songmaker Nany sacrifices. The same flower carries the identical reassuring meaning to members of a different creed: the Hindus of distant India.

Flowers delight, cure, and, in a universe that God created, have always possessed significance. In *Hamlet Prince of Denmark*, Ophelia says:

> There's rosemary, that's for remembrance. Pray you, love,
> remember.
> There is pansies, that's for thoughts....
> There's fennel for you, and columbines....

Shakespeare seems to assume that his audience was familiar with the meanings of the herbs in Ophelia's mournful posy, because she explains only the first two.

Sofonisba Anguisciola, Shakespeare's near contemporary in Italy, portrayed *A Young Lady in Profile* with a pink in hand, a flower known as a symbol of faithful love. Artist and sitter alike counted on the recipient of this portrait, whether prospective husband or distant lover, to understand what the picture conveyed. *Lady with a Pink* by Rembrandt depends upon the same visual language.

In the first half of the sixteenth century in Turkey, the official signature, or *tughra*, of the magnificent sultan Süleyman I carpeted a sweeping calligraphic emblem with carnations, symbols of the great goodness of Allah here and in the hereafter. (Perhaps the grand gesture was also a reminder to the people that God's gifts came through the sultan.)

The scientific approach informed the still life, a genre that blossomed in the seventeenth century, in works such as Ambrosius Bosschaert the Elder's *Large Bouquet in a Wan-Li Vase on Gun Metal Base* (1609). Some ten years later, Jan Brueghel the Elder painted a *Bouquet of Flowers* that glows with life, but it is an impossible picture—the flowers he portrayed grow at different times of year. Later that century, Jean-Baptiste Monnoyer became known for his floral paintings, such as *Flowers and Fruit*. In China, Shih-t'ao made ink and color drawings like *Peonies* (c. 1698), a creation of personal associations explicated in the poetry that accompanies the sensual blossoms.

The demand for still lifes was greatest among the northern European bourgeoisie. The wealthy purchased paintings of their lineage or property, or dogs. Flowers grew in hothouses in their country estates, so they could have the real thing sent to town year-round. But as the northern cities grew during the mercantile centuries, a class arose with no connection to the land. For these people, a painting was both a status symbol and a source of visual pleasure.

The seventeenth century was devastated by recurring outbreaks of the plague, and it may have been this looming dread that inspired the melancholy that is the other abiding characteristic of the age. Flowers in particular—lovely, fragile, and ephemeral—lend themselves to a commemoration of the fugitive nature of life and the vanity of life's pleasures. Rachel Ruysch's *Roses, Convolvulus, Poppies and Other Flowers in an Urn on a Stone Ledge* (c. 1745) juxtaposes flowers with the ostensibly enduring masonry of human works; against a moody, overcast background the artist has assembled a riotous composition of life, fertility, and death.

One of the most popular and sucessful portraitists of her time, Marie-Louise Élisabeth Vigée-Lebrun chose the queen of flowers, not as a symbol, but as a simile for her royal sitter: Marie-Antoinette is as splendid as a rose. The artist displayed enough of the royal bosom to make her point. Anyone close to the queen was well aware, however, that beneath the rosy breast beat the heart of a determined personality and a shrewd politician; this portrait may well have been intended to allay accusations that the queen was meddling outside her proper sphere.

Woman as ornament, lovely and fragile as a flower—this was a new notion for new economic times. Hitherto, masculine and feminine realms in all classes had most often been distinct, though not categorically so, but everyone worked, from chatelaine to cottager. Now the times were changing. Industrial wealth was accumulating, the number of domestic servants was increasing, and women—ladies—became testaments to their husbands' wealth, the more idle the better. Men's clothing became more somber, the better to set off their material success as revealed on their women's backs. Women's hands were still to be kept busy, a pretty sight, but theirs were to be the pursuits of leisure: playing the piano—but not too well—and painting, preferably delicate watercolors of flowers. Some women found other ways to express their talents: Ann Walgrave Warner's lively *Coverlet* (c. 1800) is a skilled and charming example of "women's work" with lasting value.

The nineteenth was, in Europe, the century of science. John La Farge's *Magnolia* (c. 1863) conceals scrupulous botanical observation beneath a luscious materiality. This was also the century of idealized domesticity, of carefully drawn boundaries between private and public. Inside, painters studied light and shadow, as well as the flowers that were the mark of the welcoming, well-regulated bourgeois residence.

Édouard Manet's *Peonies* (1864) exhibits a blurred form that seems almost to exude the flowers' subtle scent; with its fashionable chinoiserie decorative details, the work was sure to please. Edgar Degas' *Woman with Chrysanthemums* (1865) began as a still life; seven years later, Degas added the figure, whose autumnal dress emphasizes the flowers' season.

As the century progressed, painters referred back to their predecessors, in a series of dialogues. Hans Thoma's *Bouquet of Wild Flowers* (1872) contrasts with the magnificence of his northern European artistic forebears, as much as with the heavily upholstered rooms of his time. In an entirely different style, Paul Cézanne, too, was claiming his kinship to and his independence from the still-life tradition with his *Bouquet of Flowers in a Vase* (1873–1875). Indeed, some years later, with Picasso and Braque, Cézanne was to take the still life into unimagined realms.

Berthe Morisot's *Lady at Her Toilet* (c. 1875) also refers to a tradition, the pairing of woman and flowers, but with a resonance that carries the picture into narrative. The lady and her flowers are both seen at the end of a long society evening. The blossoms may reflect the lady, emphasizing the weariness that shows in her movement. Here, there is no metaphor for female fragility, but a realistic rendering of specific physical tiredness.

Less specific but equally affecting is *Chrysanthemums* (c. 1878), once attributed to William Merritt Chase but now thought to be the work of an unknown artist. Where Degas accentuated these flowers' season, the dark moodiness of this work recalls their association with death. They appear to have been tossed by some supernatural force—the last thing one would expect to come across in a proper middle-class sitting room.

Edith Wharton, the author of *The Age of Innocence*, also wrote *The Decoration of Houses*, a severe and sensible guide to suitable architecture and ornamentation. Wharton was most definite on the kind of art appropriate to the dining room: it should be nothing that distracts or detracts from the function for which the room is designed. Paintings of flowers and fruit are recommended as pleasing to the eye and enhancing the sociable atmosphere. At first glance, Manet's *Two Roses on a Tablecloth* (1882–1883) would seem to fit the bill, yet a second glance reveals a work that would certainly draw a diner's attention from even the finest Muscovy duck. What caused the lady absent from the picture to interrupt her serene task? Manet has turned a still life into a dramatic scene that seduces the imagination.

Henri Fantin-Latour, a vastly successful painter, sold hundreds of floral still lifes. *Bouquet of Roses and Nasturtiums in a Vase* (1883) is quite small and intimate, perhaps made for a family parlor. Martin Johnson Heade's *Giant Magnolias* (c. 1885–1895), on the other hand, seems to thrust the tropical blooms into the viewer's awareness. Painted in almost photographic detail, the painting seems to waft the magnolias' heady perfume off the canvas.

Mad, desperate, and sick, Vincent van Gogh might have carved his *Imperial Crown Fritillaries in a Copper Vase* (1886) and *Irises* (1890) out of paint and energy, feverishly experimenting with Pointillism in the first and under the influence of the Japanese master Hokusai in the second. Few images could stand in greater contrast to van Gogh's electric work than an ode to married life, *Woman at the Piano (Madame Vallotton)* painted by Félix Vallotton early in the twentieth century. The house is neat yet accommodating; Madame Vallotton has gracefully brought a little bouquet from the garden on this warm day.

Modern artists continued to prize still lifes, perhaps as much for their tradition as for the enchantment of flowers that the tide of history never diminishes. Odilon Redon worked in black and white for twenty years; among his principal influences were Edgar Allan Poe and Francisco Goya. Yet in his *Vase of Flowers* (1914), the sheer colors and prettiness of the flowers gathered by Mme Redon seem to have overwhelmed the artist, who has conveyed a sensation of all colors, of the aura of a bouquet. Henri Matisse, too, took a still life on a table, *Anemones with Black Mirror* (c. 1920)—similar to the one in Morisot's *Lady at Her Toilet*—and composed a disturbing dialogue that harkens back to Greek myth and around him to the dreadful war that was consuming Europe.

Romare Bearden is famous today for his collage scenes, alive with people and the scrupulous details of life. His *Interior* (1939) is a serene and sunny room in which the plants are flourishing proof that care is taken here. Horace Pippin's *Victorian Parlor I* (1945) bespeaks a similar domestic order, in what could be the parlor of the artist's grandparents' home. Its nostalgia is all the more poignant given the year the work was painted—the last year of World War II.

Georgia O'Keeffe's flowers, such as *Poppies* (1950), are aggressively, literally in your face—they may be womanly, but they are anything but ladylike. O'Keeffe refused interpretation, but she achieved the unique portrayal of a physical communion and commonality—joining flowers, human beings, and, by extension, the whole universe.

Flowers are also much in evidence when a death occurs, the bright loving gesture of the living. In Ellis Wilson's *Funeral Procession* (c. 1950), the posies carried by the mourners accentuate the gravity of the occasion, while recalling that life, like flowers, will always bloom again.

Unknown

Funerary Papyrus

c. 1039–991 B.C.

Painted and inscribed papyrus, 13¾"–14⅛" (34.9–35.8cm) in height.
The Metropolitan Museum of Art, New York City.

Like all Egyptian funerary texts, this papyrus (from Deir el-Bahri, an archaeological site near Thebes) combines magical spells from the *Book of the Dead* that are intended to ease the deceased's passage into the underworld. The artist chose incantations for "coming forth by day and opening the netherworld." The artist has followed tradition in making the male—the mummified Osiris, the Egyptian god of life after death—darker-skinned than the female, Nany, the subject of this papyrus, whose burial accessories were found in the tomb of Queen Meritamun in Thebes. This distinction identifies men as, literally, "outdoor types," while the woman's place, even for so aristocratic a lady as Nany, in her elaborate breastplate and transparent linen gown, was indoors. Here, Nany, a songmaker of the Twenty-first Dynasty, sacrifices to Osiris. Her offerings are meat and lotus flowers, the latter a member of the water-lily family, a traditional Egyptian and Hindu religious symbol of rebirth.

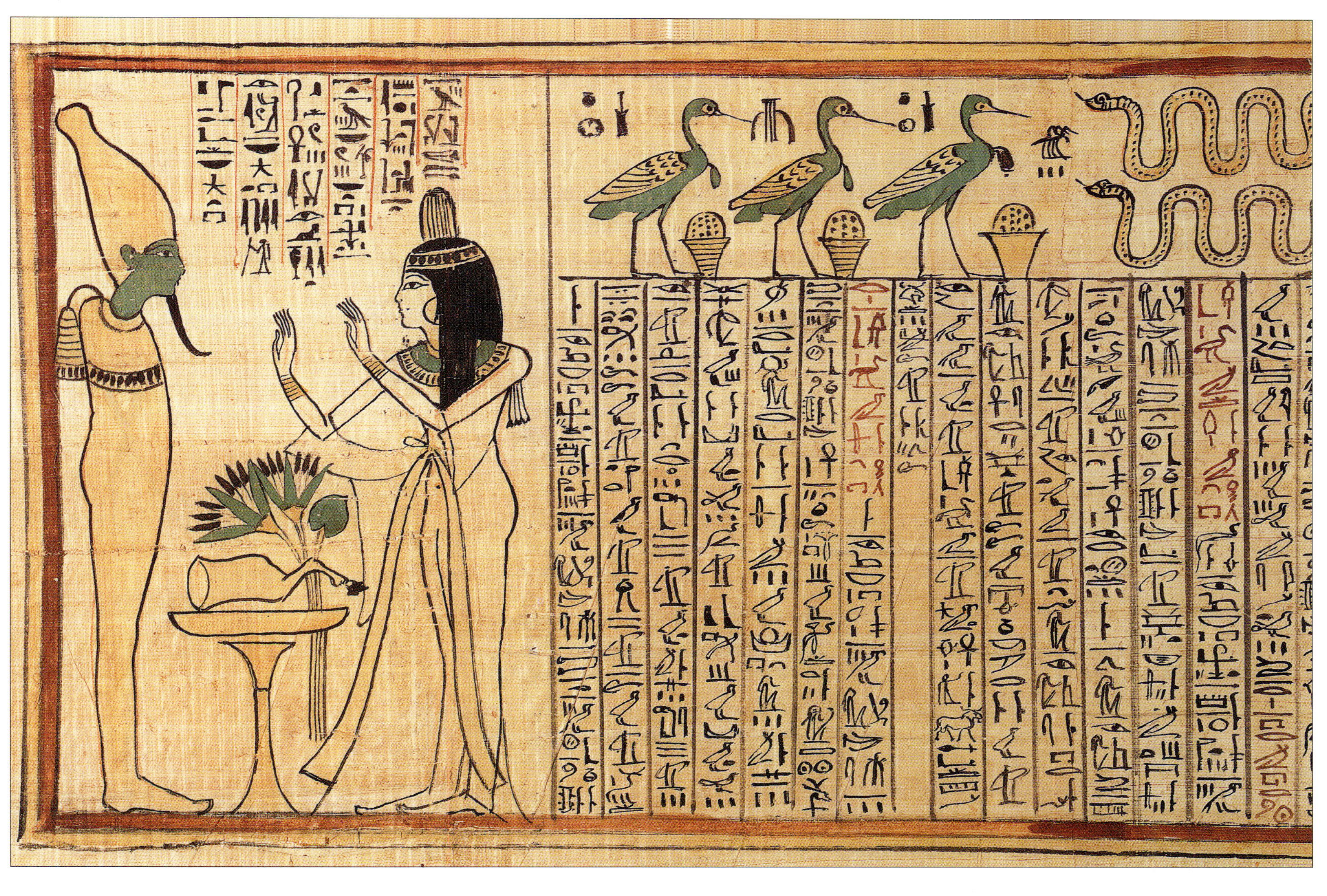

UNKNOWN

Tughra of Süleyman the Magnificent

16th century

INK, COLORS, AND GOLD ON PAPER, 20½" × 25⅜" (52.1 × 64.5CM).
THE METROPOLITAN MUSEUM OF ART, NEW YORK CITY.

Süleyman I, "the Magnificent," is still known in Turkey as "the Lawgiver." Born in 1494 or 1495, he reigned as sultan from 1520 until his death in 1566. In 1529, his military victories brought him to the gates of Vienna, and his naval might dominated the Mediterranean for a time. He reformed the administration of the Ottoman Empire, built public works, and supported the arts and sciences. The *tughra*, executed by an official, was the formal signature of the sultan. This example, a calligraphic emblem from an imperial edict of Süleyman I, is one of the finest. Calligraphy, the art of beautiful writing, was more esteemed in Islam than painting, perhaps because of the power attributed to words, specifically the words of the sacred Koran. Carnations were traditionally used by the Muslims to flavor drinks and sherbets: this simple, scented field flower, dotting the *tughra* in delightful profusion, may express the luxury, leisure, and peace of a prosperous empire; the generosity and refined goodness of its sultan; and a visual manifestation of gratitude to Allah for his grace, his bounty, and the promise of paradise.

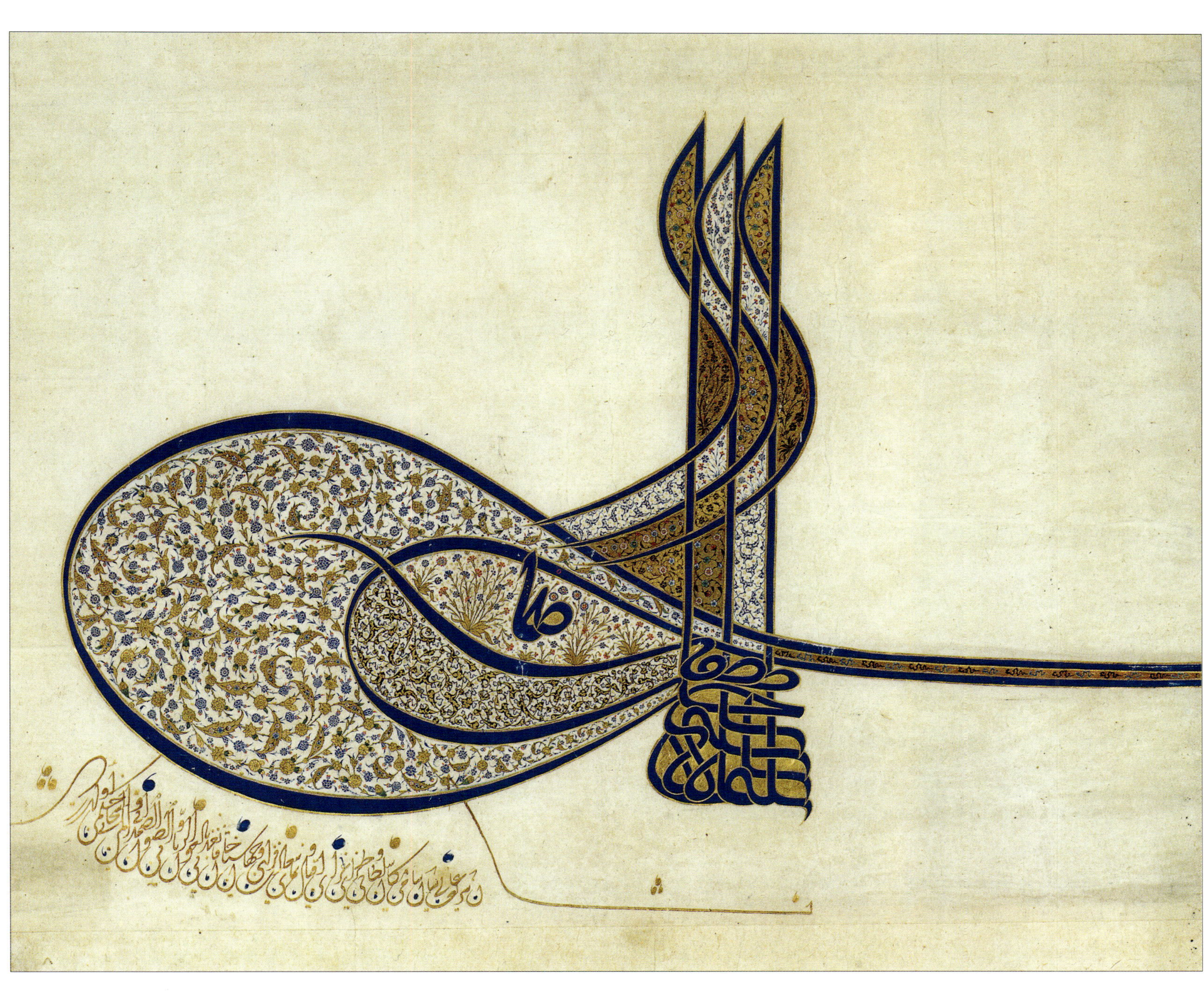

Sofonisba Anguisciola

A Young Lady in Profile

Late 16th century

Oil on canvas, 27" × 20½" (68.5 × 52cm). The Hermitage, Saint Petersburg.

Sofonisba Anguisciola (1527–1625), born near Milan, was a child when the duchy passed to the Holy Roman Emperor Charles V of Spain; the painter ended her days in Palermo, under the reign of Charles' heir, Philip II, of whom she executed a celebrated portrait. The Imperial Spanish court was notorious for its opulent formality of costume and manners, as is evident here in the portrait of a young lady. She is a noblewoman: sumptuary laws would have forbidden such rich dress to the middle classes. The heavy, dense embroidery of gold thread is accentuated by its similarity to the decoration on the vase she holds. The portrait in profile was the norm when Anguisciola made this painting, perhaps because it best exhibits the fine features considered characteristic of, and limited to, the aristocracy—a particularly important consideration when portraits were exchanged as part of a marriage negotiation. The flowers are pinks, of the same family as carnations, and an educated European viewer would have read their meaning as faithful love. But whether this floral note was intended to render the unknown sitter more attractive to a prospective husband, or as a remembrance to a distant lover, we shall never know.

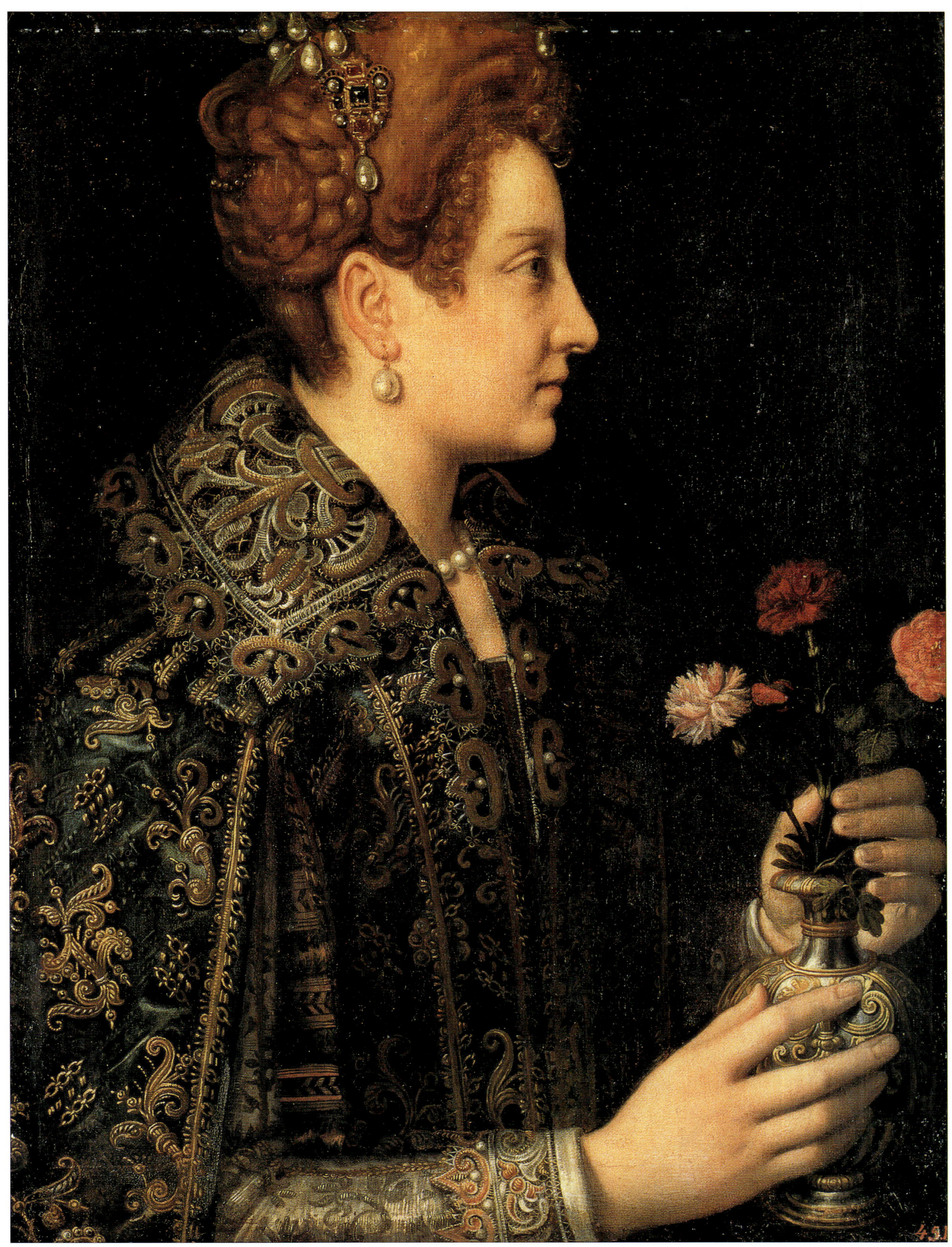
431

Ambrosius Bosschaert the Elder

Large Bouquet in a Wan-Li Vase on Gun Metal Base

1609

Oil on mahogany panel, 19$\frac{13}{16}$" × 14" (50.3 × 35.5cm). Kunsthistorisches Museum, Vienna.

After the Reformation, northern Europe experienced a growing public demand for beautiful, secular paintings. Ambrosius Bosschaert the Elder (1573–1621) was one of the Dutch artists who successfully satisfied this new desire. Neither the Catholic Church nor pious private citizens were commissioning religious works in the Calvinist North, but Bosschaert and others found patrons among the emerging and very prosperous middle-class merchants, such as those who imported vases like this one from China. There is nothing naturalistic in these perfect, theatrical specimens that glow with inner life—caterpillars notwithstanding. In the vivacious, almost coquettish arabesques of the artist's lines, these flowers far surpass any real ones that aristocrats might have brought into their town or country houses from gardens and conservatories. The splendid flowers painted by this artist and his peers no longer resonate with Catholic symbolism, though they still carry moral associations. For example, the tulip that is so present in seventeenth-century Dutch works may serve as a reminder of the dangers of fiscal intemperance: that flower, first imported from the Near East in the late sixteenth century, rapidly became the object of speculation so extreme that it is still cited in today's financial journals. It was not unheard of for Dutch farmers to trade an entire farm for one tulip bulb.

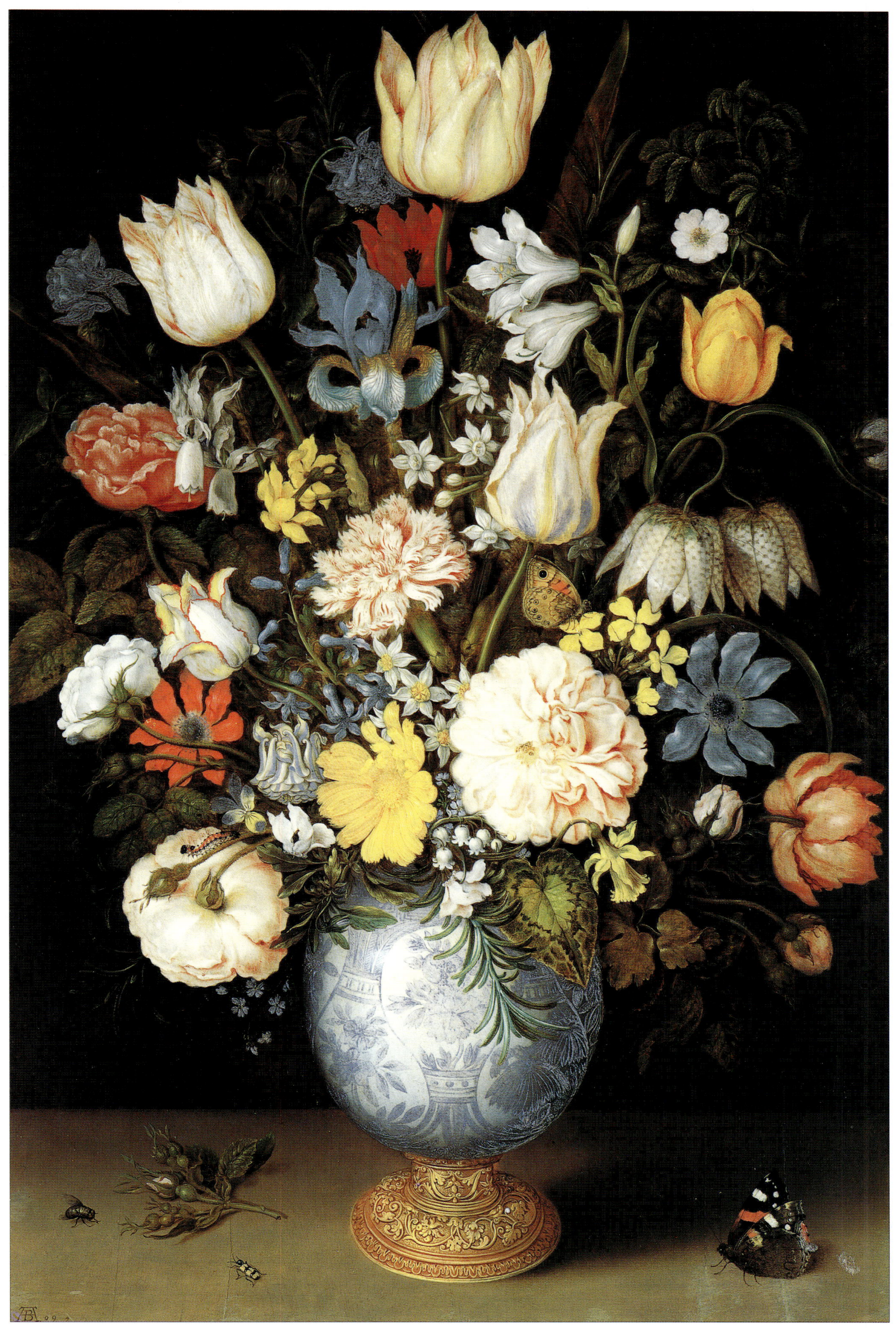

Jacob Jordaens

Madonna and Child Wreathed with Flowers

c. 1618

Oil on canvas, 41" × 29" (104.1 × 73.6cm). The Hermitage, Saint Petersburg.

Jacob Jordaens (1593–1678) was a painter of portraits, scenes of daily life in Flanders, and historical, religious, and mythological subjects. He also painted murals and designed tapestries. His strength was a modest yet full-hearted style, evident in this delicate but richly colored image of Madonna and Child. The history of Christian art is one of increasing humanization, parallel to the evolution of theological dogma. This development is chiefly visible in the faces of the personages, which become more expressive, less hieratic, even when the surroundings are lavish, as they are more often in Italy than in northern Europe. Yet as private as this mother and child are, Jordaens followed traditional iconography in his foreshadowing of the role the Christ Child will play in eternity: the babe points up with one hand and down with the other, for it is he who will judge on the last day, choosing who will rise to join the saints and who will descend to the lower darkness. Perhaps the nineteenth-century painter Andris Daniels found Jordaens' representation too humble: he added the wide garland of flowers, traditionally associated with the Virgin, to emphasize her fulfillment of her maternal role.

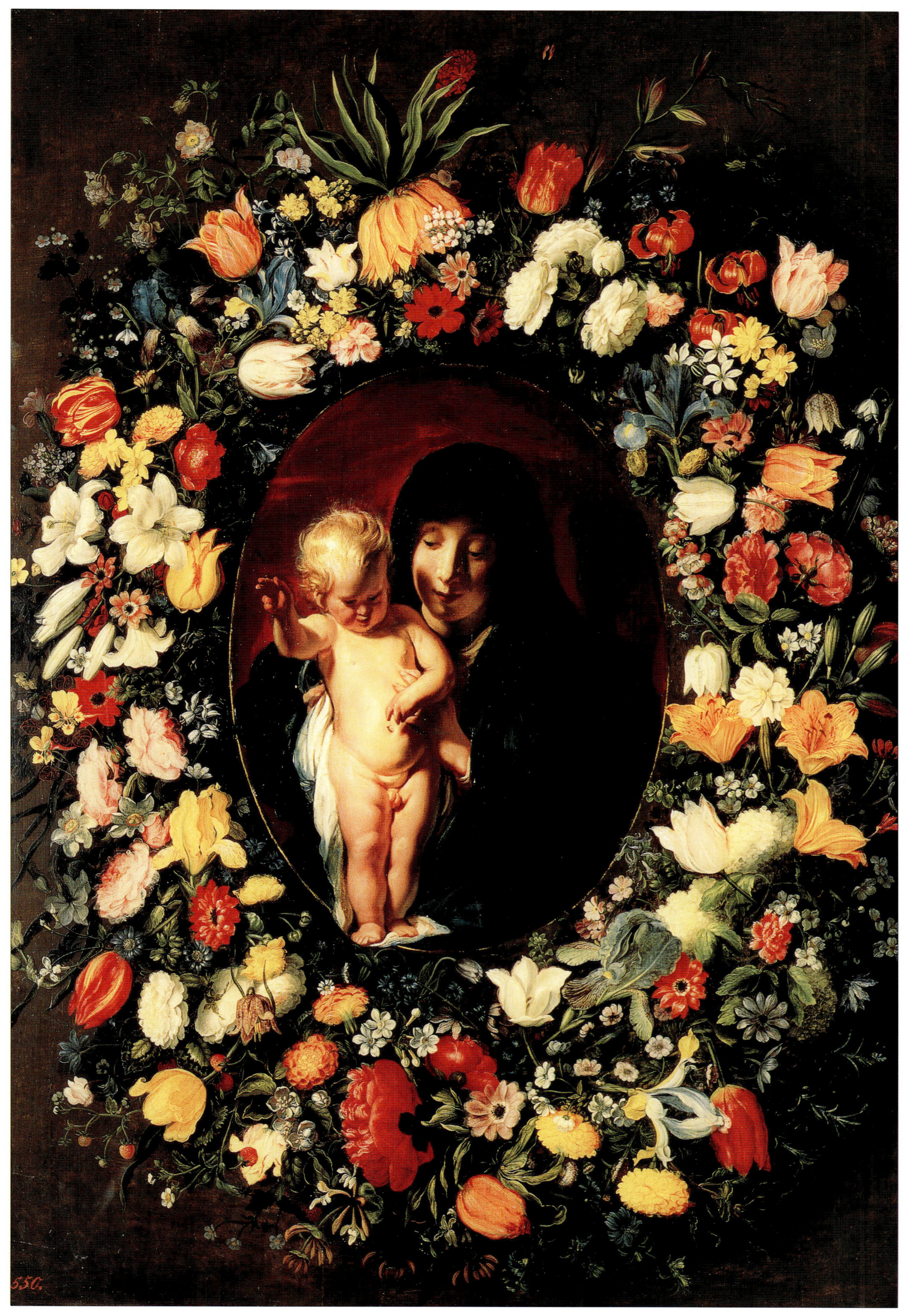
550.

Rembrandt

Lady with a Pink

Mid- to late 17th century

Oil on canvas, 36¼" × 29⅜" (92.1 × 74.6cm). The Metropolitan Museum of Art, New York City.

Painter, etcher, and draftsman, Rembrandt (1606–1669) settled in Amsterdam as a portraitist and teacher in 1631. Three years later, he married a wealthy woman, Saskia van Uylenburgh, and executed numerous portraits of her and of their son, Titus, as well as many self-portraits. Saskia died in 1642; by 1656, this master of light and shadow was declared bankrupt, despite his preeminence in the Dutch school of painting and his prolific output of portraits and of religious and mythological subjects. (Of his drawings alone, more than sixteen hundred survive.) Here, the artist used light to create a mystical effect—a luminous air around the pink, a flower related to the carnation and a traditional European pictorial emblem of faithful love. This woman of wealth and fashion, her complex humanity accentuated by the severe angle of the gilded and formal frame behind her, is literally lost in a brown study. The deep red of her gown evokes the depth and dignity of her passion, and subtly sets off the vibrant, vivid rose color of the flower.

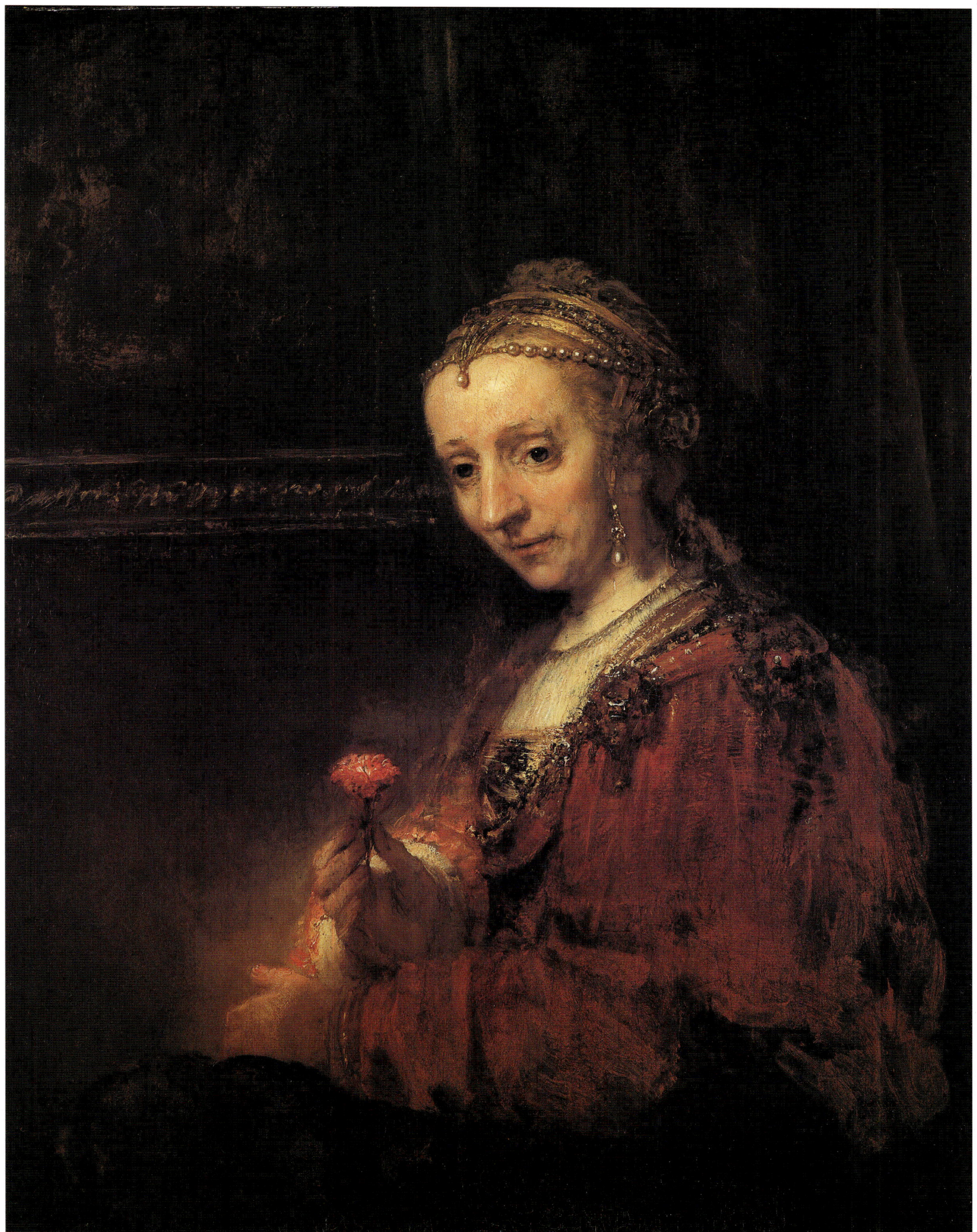

Jean-Baptiste Monnoyer

Flowers and Fruit

Mid- to late 17th century

Oil on canvas, 29" × 48" (73.6 × 121.9cm). The Hermitage, Saint Petersburg.

This gloomy work may have been one of four, painted for the area over the doors in a dining room. Jean-Baptiste Monnoyer (1634–1699) was well known for his pictures of flowers, and was active in the decoration of Versailles and the Trianon, among royal residences in France, and of Montagu House and the Kensington and Hampton Court palaces in England. True to the melancholy period that had witnessed the Great Plague rage through London in 1665 and 1666, this mournful still life celebrates the transience of power and of worldly pleasures, the overturned silver urn taking the place previously held by a cornucopia in classical art. There is nothing of the conventional sighing over the ephemeral nature of human life here; instead, a heartfelt anxiety is evident in the brush strokes and dramatic contrast of light and dark. Poppies are the flower of Morpheus, the Greek god of dreams, and Monnoyer would not be the first to opine that life is a dream. This reminder of the vanity of earthly things harks back to the triumphs of the Roman emperors; in the midst of lavish victory processions, the emperor kept beside him a servant whose duty was to whisper, "*Memento mori*"—Remember that you will die.

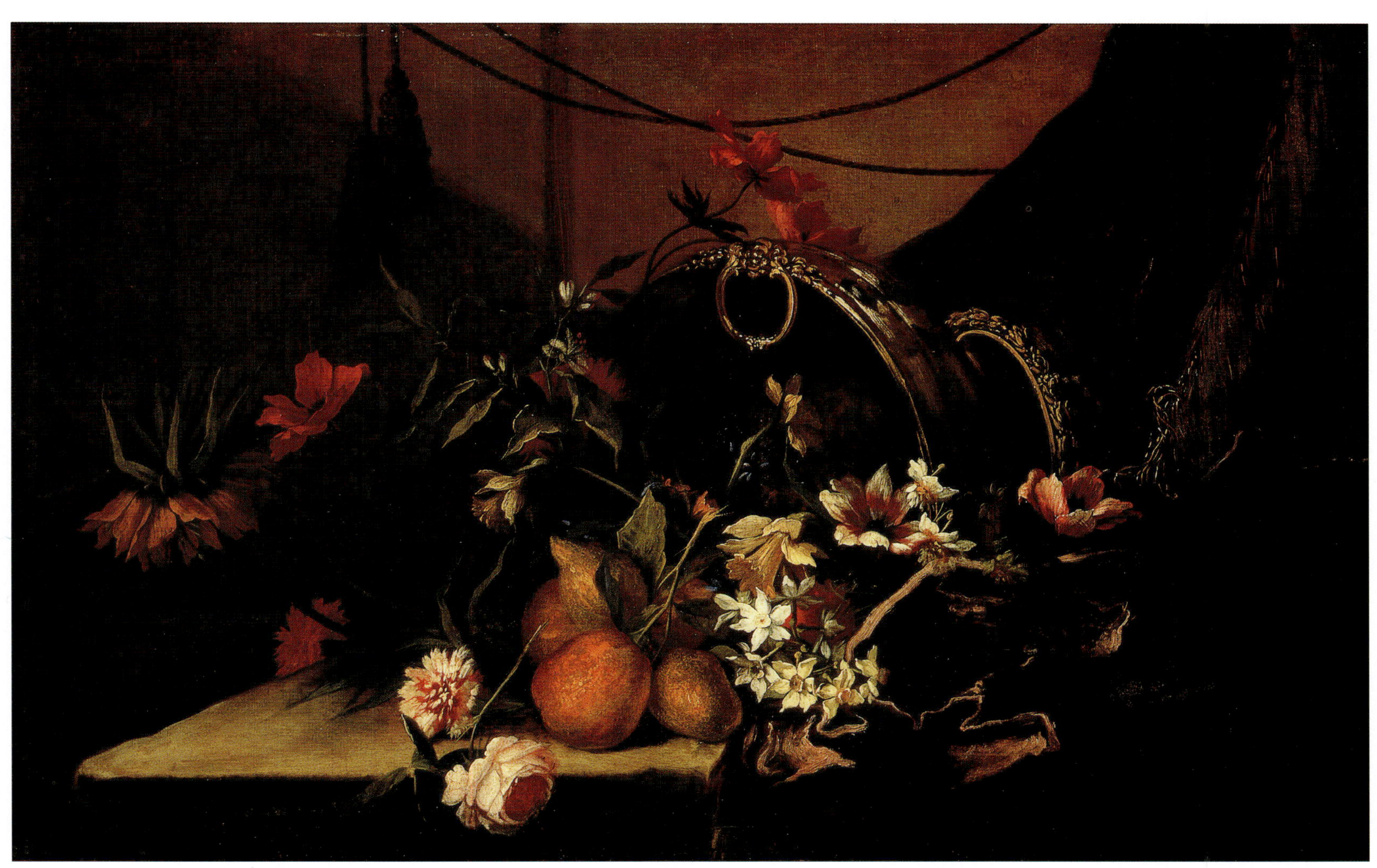

Elisabetta Sirani

Virgin and Child

1663

Oil on canvas, 34" × 27½" (86.3 × 69.8cm). The National Museum of Women in the Arts, Washington, D.C.

In her short life (she may have died of ulcers, though it was rumored that her maid poisoned her), Elisabetta Sirani (1638–1665) was a prolific and successful artist who fulfilled numerous private commissions as well as some public works. True to her time, Sirani painted religious, allegorical, historical, and mythological subjects. Breaking from the hieratic, gilded theatricality of the previous century, here she has portrayed the Madonna and Child in an intimately tender scene. Their identities in eternity are encoded: though a would-be coarse brown fabric swathes Mary's head and shoulders, she wears her traditional blue cloak. The child is seated on a princely cushion, and Mary does not touch her son directly. Finally—a foretelling, perhaps, of his future assumption of her into heaven—the babe crowns his mother with a wreath of roselike carnations (white for the Virgin birth and red for Christ's passion), which casts its shadow of loss and glory over this moment of humble human joy.

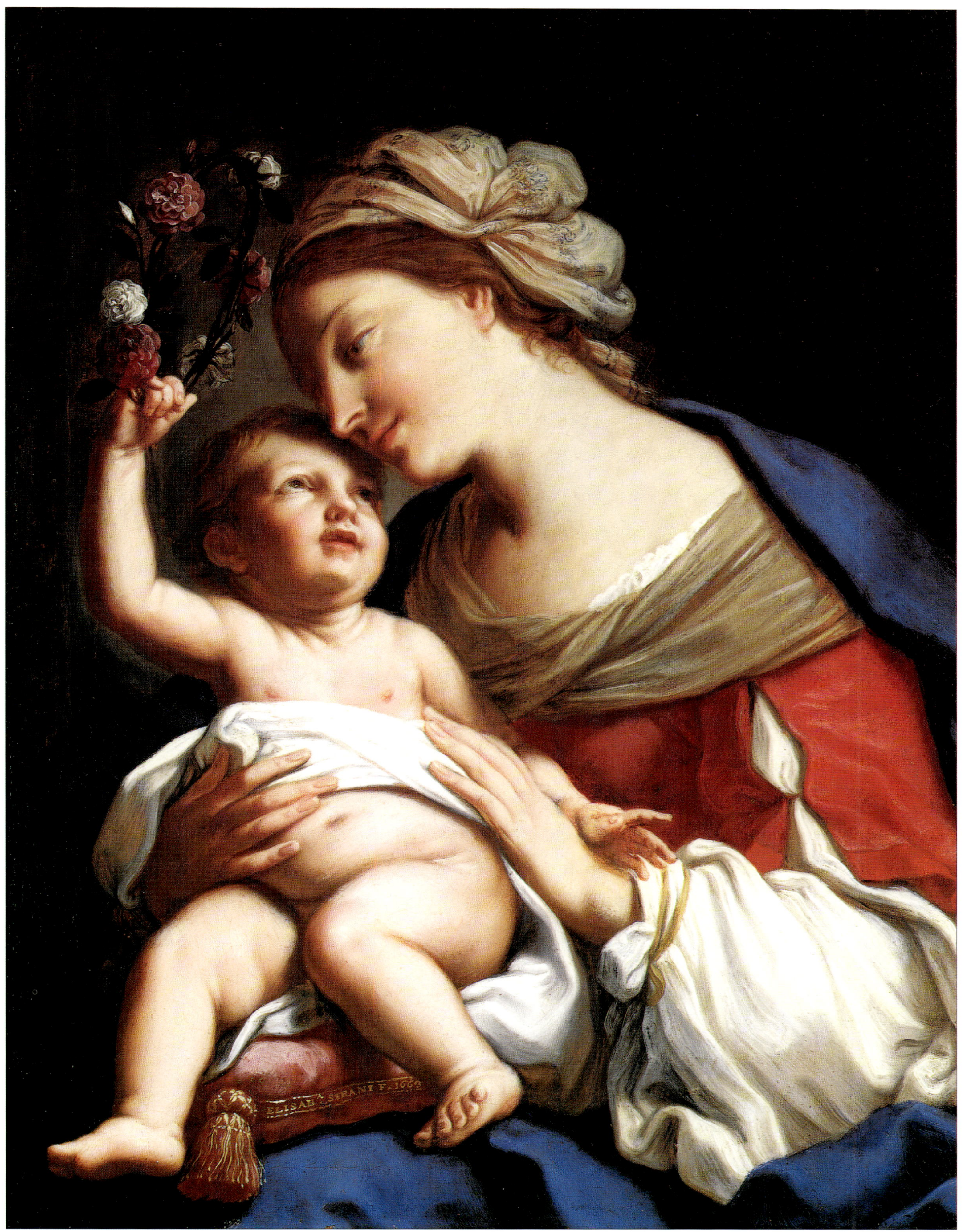
ELISAB^A SERANI F. 1663

SHIH-T'AO

Peonies

c. 1698

LEAF D FROM AN ALBUM OF NINE LEAVES, INK AND COLOR ON PAPER. THE ARTHUR M. SACKLER COLLECTION, NEW YORK.

Shih-t'ao (1642–c. 1707) lived his adult life under the reign of the emperor Hsüan-yeh, second of the Ch'ing dynasty. Hsüan-yeh was a ruler of vision, a diplomat, and a patron of the arts, and in his time a group of painters known as the Individualists flourished. One of the most famous was Shih-t'ao, a Buddhist monk, traveler, and courtier. He painted in a number of styles, but always sought to capture, in the images of flowers that comprised much of his work, a wanton, almost giddy elation. A monk during his youth, Shih-t'ao only returned to the world after he was fifty, and in his later years he expressed in poetry his intensely personal and sensual associations with specific blossoms—scents, textures, and tender, natural metaphors for lovemaking. In the ten years before he died, the artist painted an album entitled *Flowers*, which included this portrait of tree peonies. The calligraphic lines of the accompanying verses exhibit the same contrast as the lines of the drawing: "After rain they radiate a beauty that can overthrow a city…."

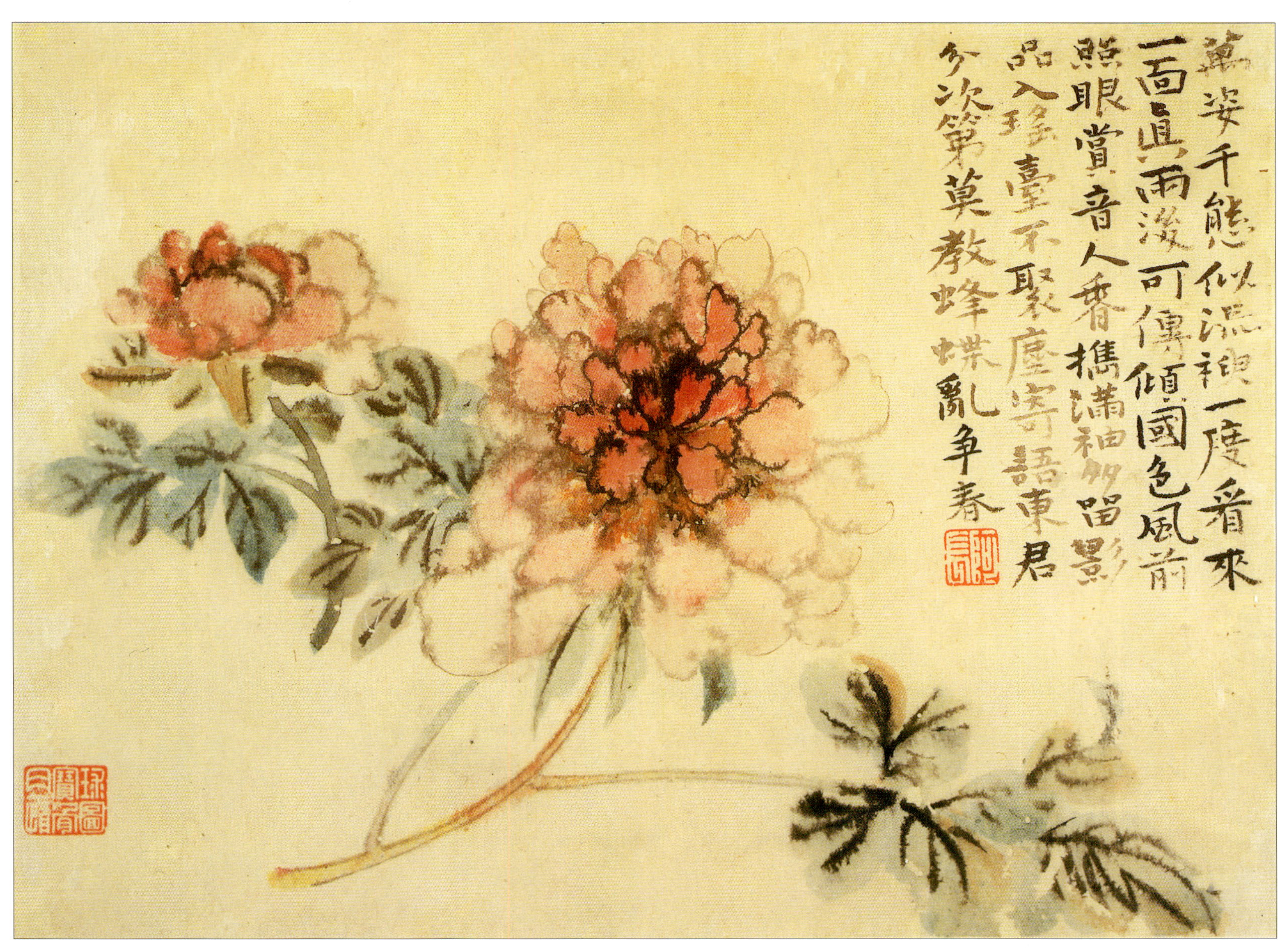

RACHEL RUYSCH

Roses, Convolvulus, Poppies and Other Flowers in an Urn on a Stone Ledge

c. 1745

OIL ON CANVAS, 42½" × 33" (108 × 83.8CM). THE NATIONAL MUSEUM OF WOMEN IN THE ARTS, WASHINGTON, D.C.

By the time Rachel Ruysch (1664–1750) painted this extravagant collection of brilliant flowers, several currents in European culture had converged. Still lifes, once the visual expressions of a melancholy obsession with death and with the passing of earthly beauty, had become ornamental portrayals that reflected the owner's sensibilities. The convention survives in the contrast between the resplendent blooms and the dark, moody architecture that frames them. The humanism of the Renaissance had also inspired a scientific view of nature, evident in precise botanical renderings. Ruysch, famous for paintings of fruits, insects, and reptiles, as well as of flowers, was the daughter of an anatomist and botanist and the granddaughter of an architect—influences we can see here. Finally, in a development most noticeable in northern Europe, a new class had arisen, a prosperous urban class of merchants with no ties to the land and therefore no source of fresh flowers, yet prosperous enough to commission paintings of them. Ruysch, apprenticed to a painter at fifteen, was extremely successful, and was the first woman to become famous as an artist on both sides of the Atlantic. She married in 1693, and though she bore ten children, she executed at least one hundred paintings. In 1708 she was appointed court painter by the Düsseldorf Elector Palatine.

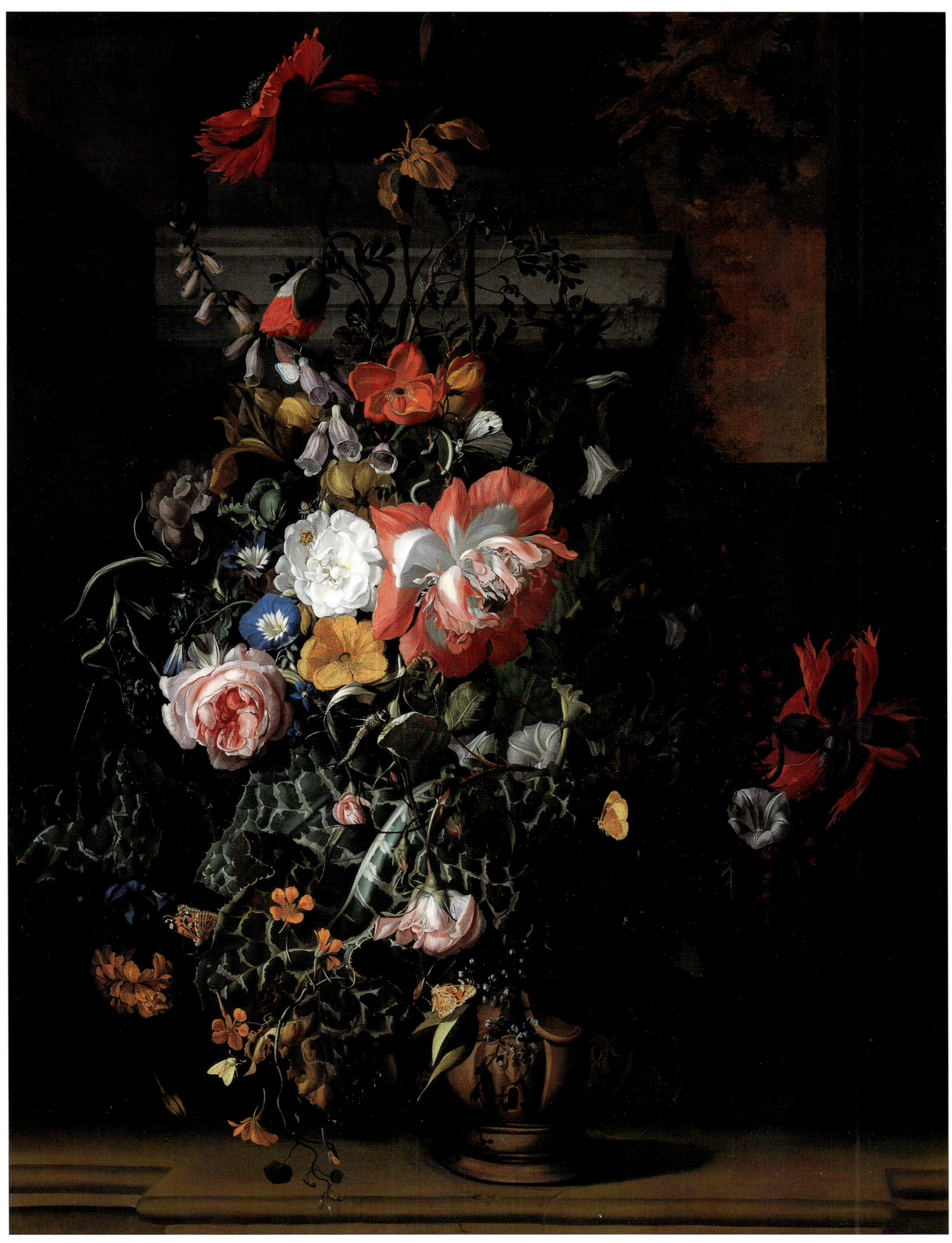

MARIE-LOUISE ÉLISABETH VIGÉE-LEBRUN

Marie-Antoinette

1783

OIL ON CANVAS, 45" × 35" (113 × 87CM). CHÂTEAU DE VERSAILLES, FRANCE.

Marie-Louise-Élisabeth Vigée-Lebrun (1755–1842) was one of the most celebrated portrait painters of the late eighteenth century. The daughter of an artist, she was rigorously trained, and was licensed as a master painter by the time she was nineteen. She received her first royal commission some two years later and made a career portraying the nobility: this painting is one of more than twenty that Vigée-Lebrun executed of Marie-Antoinette. In 1789, this successful artist left France and the winds of revolutionary change for England, where she was once again received by the highest nobility. She has left portraits from this period of Lady Hamilton, Lord Byron, and two English princesses, among others. Her works are courtly yet insightful. Here, for example, Vigée-Lebrun uses simile to represent the Queen of France: Marie-Antoinette is like a rose. By conforming to conventional comparisons of a lady with a flower—beautiful, delicate, and born to please—the artist may have been defending her patron from vitriolic factional accusations of politicking. The slight mauve tint of the blossom only serves to enhance the creamy feminine rosiness of the queen's face, bosom, and arms. Her high-born delicacy demands that a silk ribbon protect her dainty fingers from the rose's thorns. History turned out to be less protective.

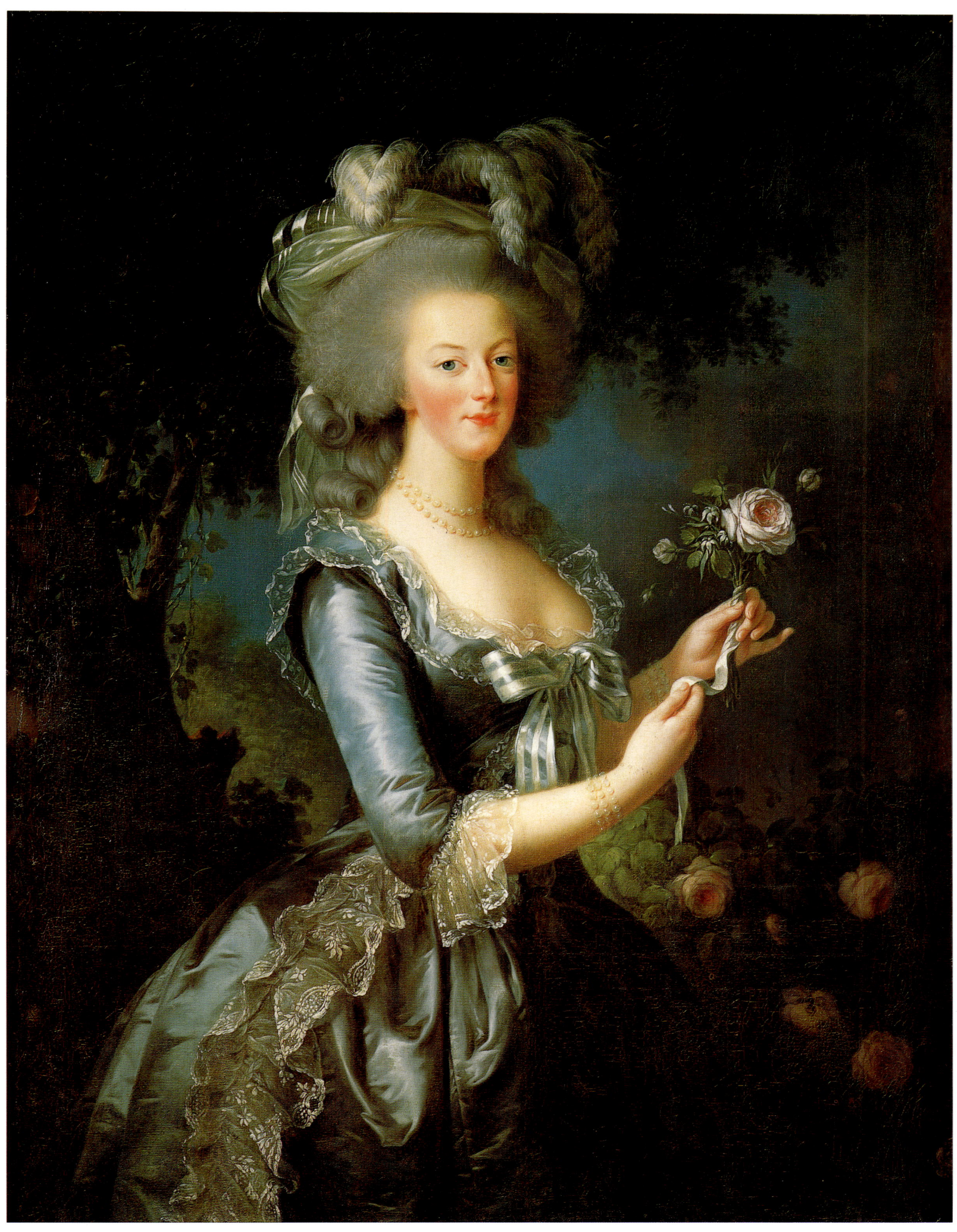

Ann Walgrave Warner

Coverlet

c. 1800

Linen and cotton, 104" × 90" (264.2 × 228.6cm). The Metropolitan Museum of Art, New York City.

At the end of the eighteenth century in North America, it was still considered seemly for the lady of even a prosperous household to be industrious, for many believed that idle hands made work for the Devil. While her husband read, perhaps out loud to the family, a gently bred wife and mother might stitch an elegant coverlet such as this one—a not-so-distant cousin of the patchwork quilts designed and assembled from scraps in humbler homes. Mothers made these for daughters about to be married, and for friends leaving, often forever. Ann Walgrave Warner stitched this one for her daughter Phebe. The combination of linen and cotton is intriguing: linen was still widely used for most of the items for which cotton is used today; in fact, it is still considered finer, more suited to sensitive skin. Hemp was also a popular textile, but in 1800, about the time this coverlet was made, cotton was beginning to appear in the United States in significant quantities. The design of flowers is historically associated with women, perhaps because beauty and fragility were conventionally desirable traits in girls and women in much of the world. Some of these flowers are in baskets; might this be a mother's wish—that her daughter be safely cradled in a loving marriage?

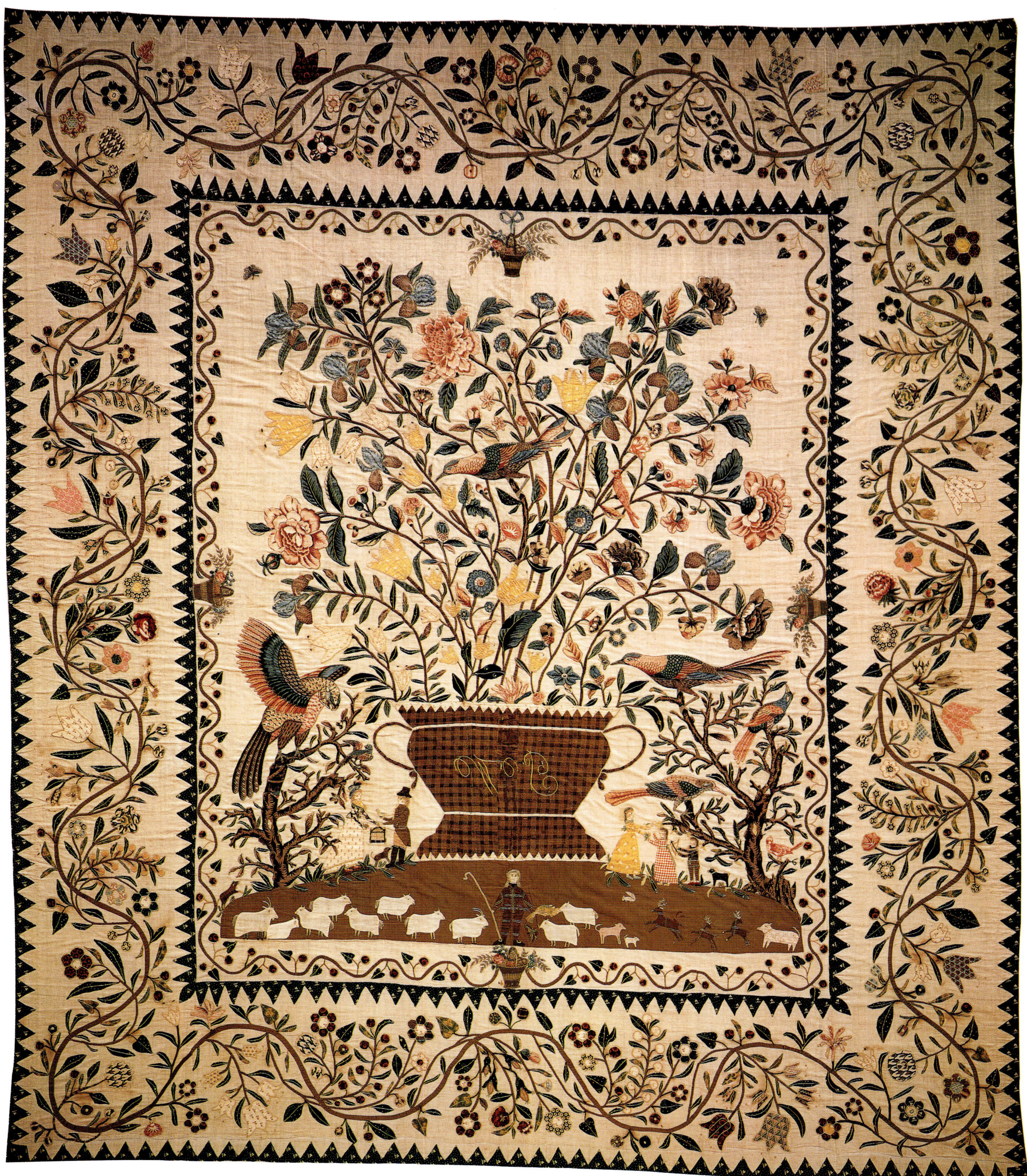

John La Farge

Magnolia

c. 1863

Oil on panel, 16" × 11¼" (40.6 × 28.5cm). The Berkshire Museum, Pittsfield, Massachusetts.

From the mid-1870s on, the American artist John La Farge (1835–1910) became increasingly prominent as a decorative artist, executing commissions for a number of important panels and stained glass windows on the East Coast and in the Midwest, as well as designs for tombs and other projects, large and small. In the first period of his career, however, beginning in about 1860, La Farge principally painted landscapes and flowers. These were very popular with the art-buying public, perhaps because of the seamless skill with which La Farge joined botanical realism to a powerfully expressive, even dramatic presentation. He particularly liked this painting, done when he was in his late twenties. In keeping with the moody and spiritually complex Pre-Raphaelite aesthetic, the lighting, the brushwork visible on the cloth on which the bowl and flower rest, and the unexpected close-up effect combine to suggest (barely) contained tempestuous passions. The picture is anything but a still life, becoming instead a symbol for the tenuously harnessed forces of nature, human and otherwise.

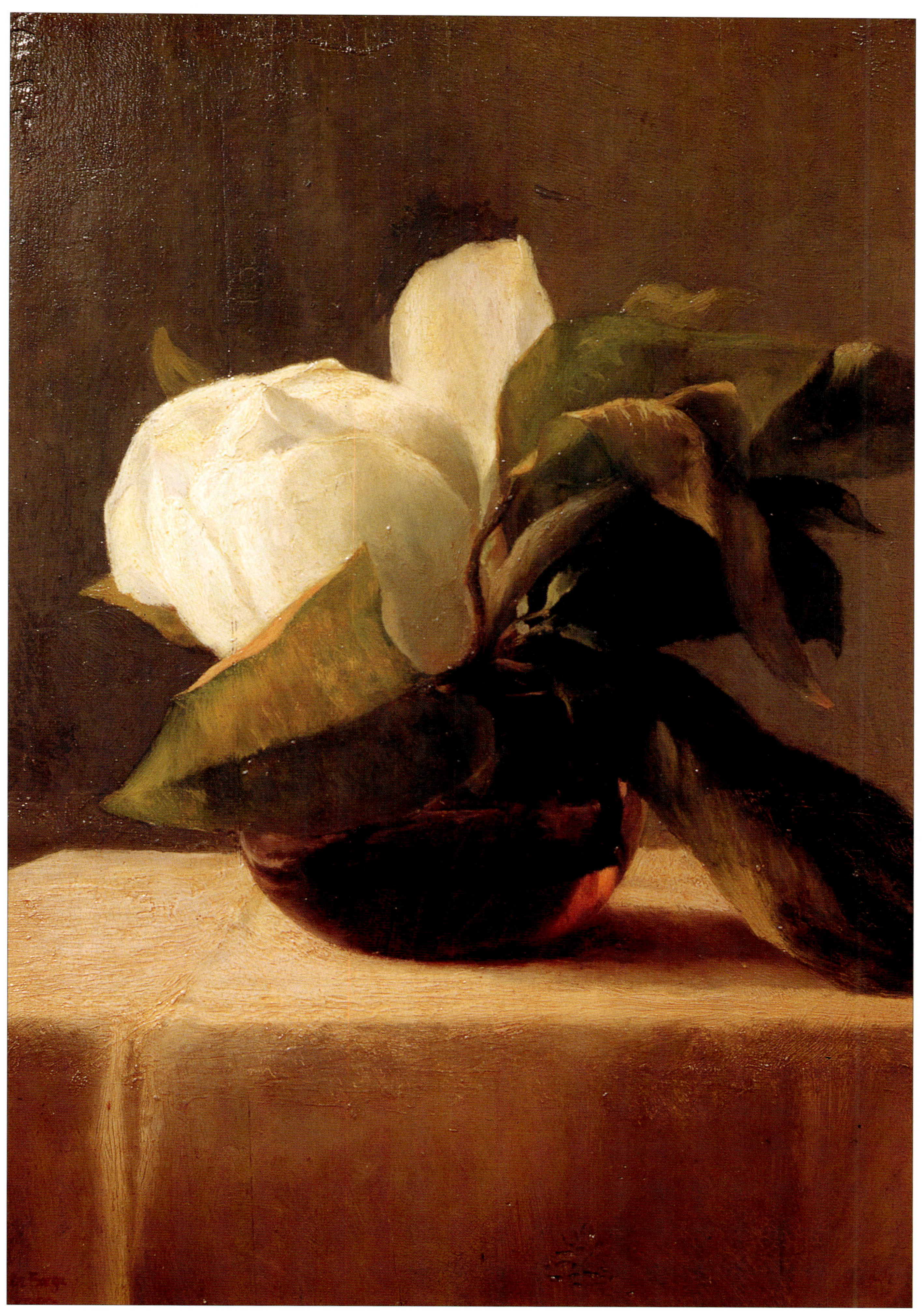

Édouard Manet

Peonies

1864

Oil on canvas, 23⅜" × 13⅞" (59.4 × 35.2cm). The Metropolitan Museum of Art, New York City.

The work of Édouard Manet (1832–1883) was enormously influential on the painters who became the Impressionists. The year after Manet scandalized Parisian society with his painting *Déjeuner sur l'herbe*, in which a classical nude sheds all sense of formality, becoming frankly and casually naked, the artist painted this glowing bouquet. The blurred forms seem redolent with the flowers' fragrance. By Manet's time, commissioned works were no longer the norm; but the bohemian artists' freedom to paint what they wished—a model we take for granted today—was purchased at the price of financial insecurity. This was certainly true in Manet's case, even though he, like a number of his colleagues, enjoyed a small private income. This quiet still life has overtones of the popular chinoiserie, or Chinese, style, evident in the red lacquered tray; the warm gray background emphasizes the hues of blossoms and leaves. This work must have easily found a buyer, perhaps among the city dwellers far from their country-house gardens, and so brought the wonders of nature indoors.

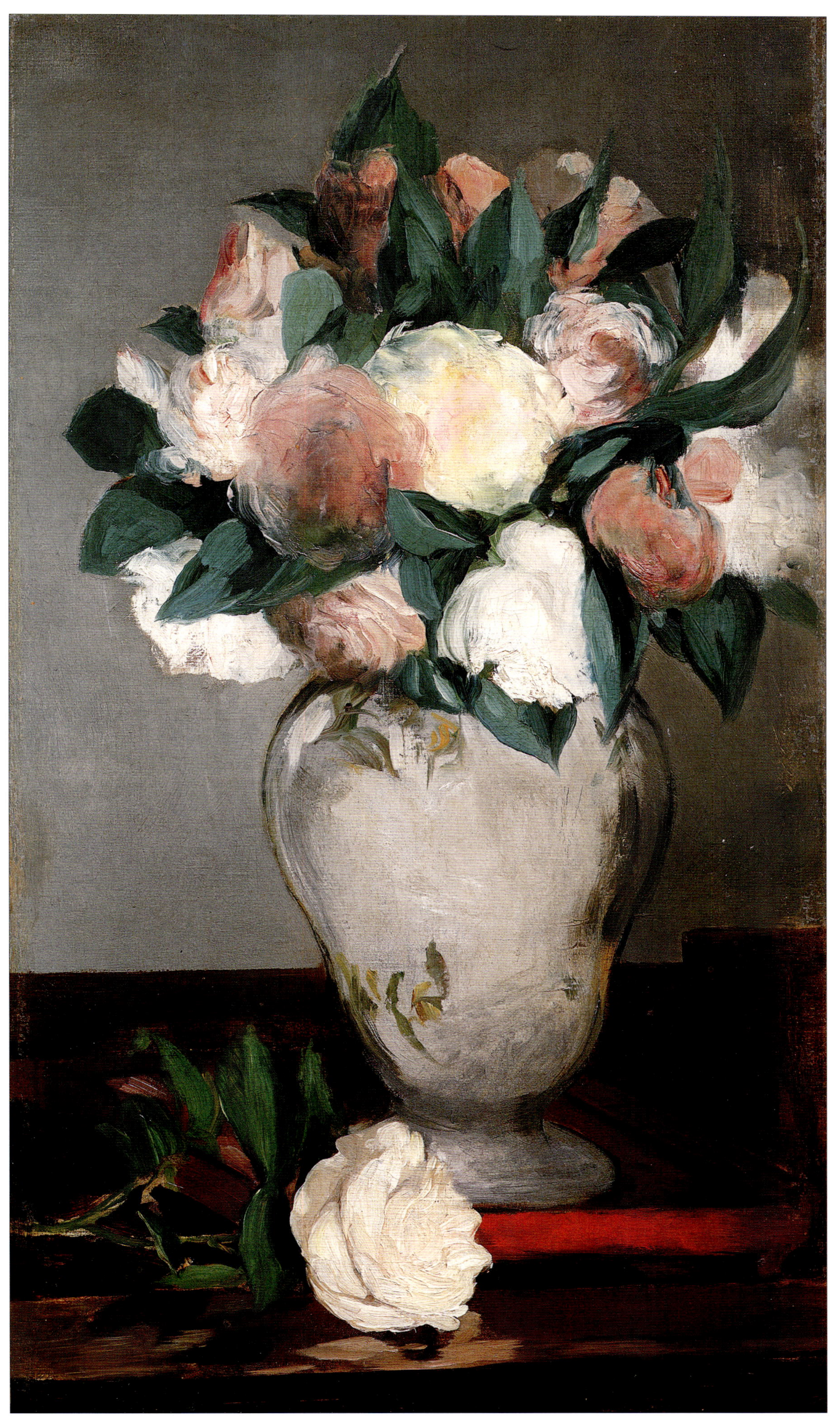

Edgar Degas

Woman with Chrysanthemums

1865

Oil on canvas, 29" × 36½" (73.7 × 92.7cm). The Metropolitan Museum of Art, New York City.

Originally an 1858 still life of autumn flowers (actually asters, not chrysanthemums), this painting did not include the figure (who may be Madame Paul Valpinçon) until seven years later. The woman's dress, in two tones of brown, is appropriate to the season; her thoughtful, inward-looking expression also seems apt for the time when nature goes underground. Edgar Degas (1834–1917) is best known for his paintings of figures in motion, whether horses at the track or ballet dancers at work and behind the scenes. Like a number of fellow artists, such as Henri de Toulouse-Lautrec and Édouard Manet, Degas explored nonacademic, "low" subjects. But where Manet leveled the moral playing field for women and men, revealing social and commercial negotiations between existential peers, and Toulouse-Lautrec emphasized the transgressive energy of cancan dancers and singers in smoky boîtes, Degas maintained the double standard—and double life—of the traditional boulevardier, the man-about-town. The gentleman who depicted this proper lady would in later years choose other objects for his gaze and artistic purposes—horses, dancers, and the vilified denizens of the brothels he frequented.

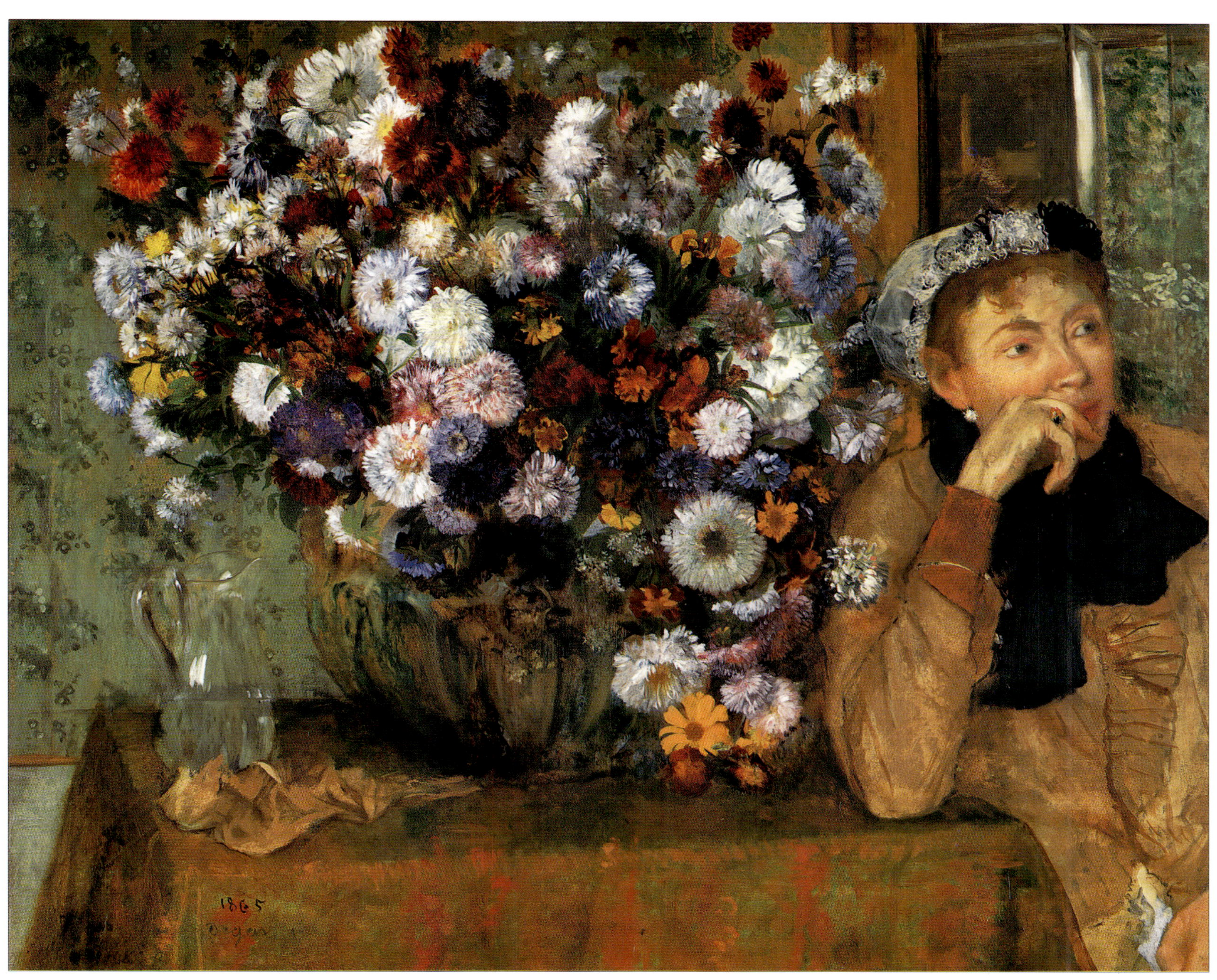

HANS THOMA

Bouquet of Wild Flowers

1872

OIL ON CANVAS, 29½" × 21⅝" (75 × 55CM).
PREUSSICHES KULTURBESITZ, NATIONALGALERIE, STAATLICHE MUSEEN ZU BERLIN.

There is no biological distinction between plants that grow wild and those cultivated in the garden, yet wildflowers have connotations all their own. Gathering wildflowers takes us, literally, off the beaten path into the riot of nature. Out there, with so many senses coming into play, we may feel more truly—and more simply—ourselves, enjoying the serendipity of the blossoms at hand. The German artist Hans Thoma (1839–1924) painted landscapes, genre scenes, portraits, and religious and allegorical subjects, all of which have historically used flowers to enhance their meaning and beauty. He was a lithographer, etcher, and illustrator, as well as a painter. Referring to a tradition of realistic flower painting that prizes spectacular effects, Thoma may be reminding us, with this modest yet enchanting bouquet, of the lilies of the field: "...they toil not, neither do they spin. Even Solomon in all his glory was not arrayed like one of these." (Matthew 6:28–29)

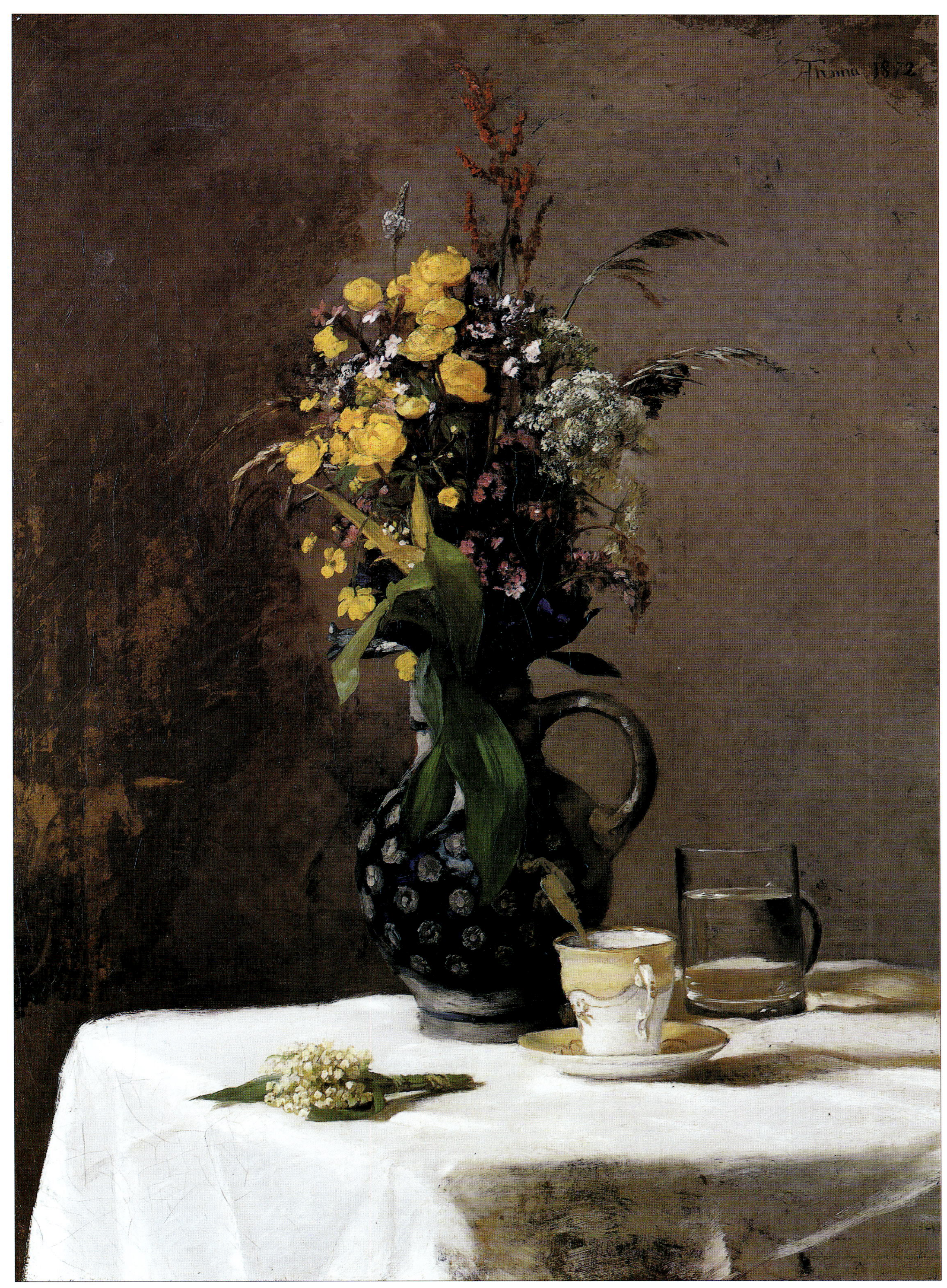
AThoma 1872

Paul Cézanne

Bouquet of Flowers in a Vase

1873–1875

Oil on canvas, 22" × 18" (56 × 46cm). The Hermitage, Saint Petersburg.

At the time he executed this still life, Paul Cézanne (1839–1906), considered one of the earliest theoreticians of modern painting, was frequenting the studios of the Impressionists, especially Camille Pissarro, Claude Monet, and Pierre-Auguste Renoir. There is an intimation of the magician giving away the tricks in this radiant work in which the brush strokes are so clear, the impasto (the matter of the pigment) so thick and lustrous. The sober, near-periwinkle color of the vase sets off the exuberant mix of tones in the bouquet, the whole resting on an earth brown surface and backed by a sun yellow wall. We can follow the shadow of the vase on the unspecified surface and infer a patch of light to its right. The artist has portrayed real flowers and greenery, but has transmuted them by Impressionist alchemy into rich, sure distillations of colors.

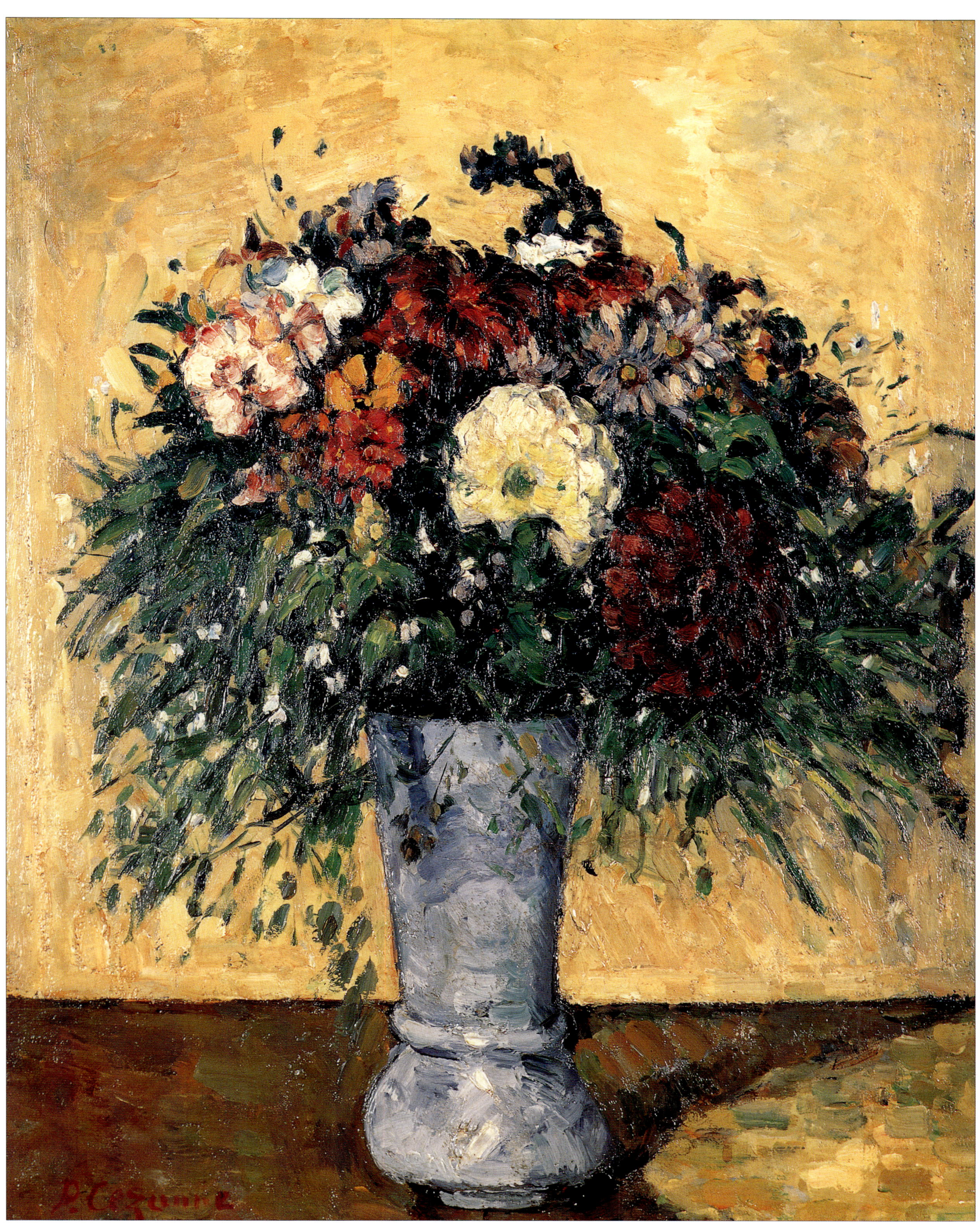

Berthe Morisot

Lady at Her Toilet

c. 1875

Oil on canvas, 23¾" × 31½" (60.3 × 80.4cm). The Stickney Fund, Art Institute of Chicago.

Berthe Morisot (1841–1895), a granddaughter of the successful painter Jean-Honoré Fragonard, studied at the Louvre, and, beginning in 1860, with Camille Corot, became a precursor of the Impressionists. Her work appeared at the Salon in 1864 and for ten years after, until she joined the Impressionists Claude Monet, Camille Pissarro, and Édouard Manet. (When Morisot married Eugène Manet, Édouard's brother, their home became an informal salon frequented by artists and intellectuals.) In 1877 she showed at the first exhibition to be labeled "Impressionist." Noted for their delicate coloration, Morisot's paintings also have an understated narrative content. Here, the woman is most likely taking down her hair after a social night out—perhaps so late that she has sent her lady's maid to bed. Her posture is relaxed and a little tired; one shoulder strap has slipped after the evening's exertions, and the flowers may be a sweet memento—or simply one of the props that the business of society requires of women. Though the history of art includes many paintings of women before mirrors, here is neither vanity nor seduction but rather one of the intimate, emotionally true moments of life that Morisot excelled in depicting.

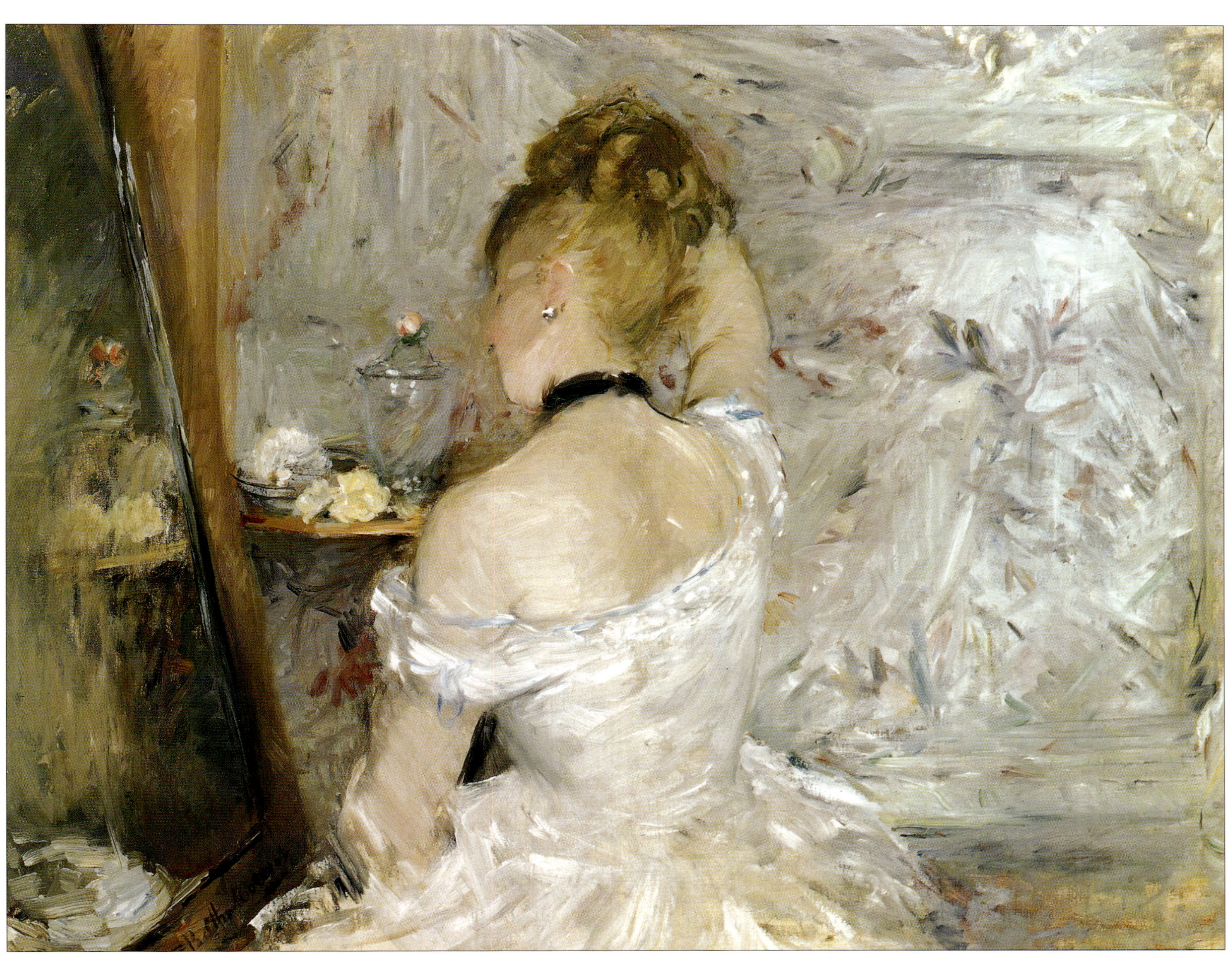

UNKNOWN

Chrysanthemums

Fourth quarter 19th century

OIL ON CANVAS, 26⅞" × 44¾" (68.2 × 113.7CM). NATIONAL GALLERY OF ART, WASHINGTON, D.C.

The artistic movement known as Impressionism is as remarkable for the diversity of styles it accommodates as for its practitioners' achievement of making realistic pictures with distinguishable brush strokes. Most often associated with plein air, light-washed exteriors, Impressionism was easily adapted to interiors, as is evident in the works of Mary Cassatt, Édouard Manet, and Berthe Morisot, among others. But where some Impressionists conveyed sensations, that is, their perceptions of the effects of light, this painting, which was once attributed to William Merritt Chase (1849–1916), seems to be projecting a moodiness onto the chrysanthemums themselves—what literature calls the pathetic fallacy. These autumn flowers, which in Europe are traditionally associated with death, appear to have been hit by some turbulent force of nature that has caused their petals to scatter, depicted with anxious brush strokes like those of the leaves. There is something exhausted about the effect of the whole: nothing could be further from the sunny, serene arrangements typical of bourgeois salons.

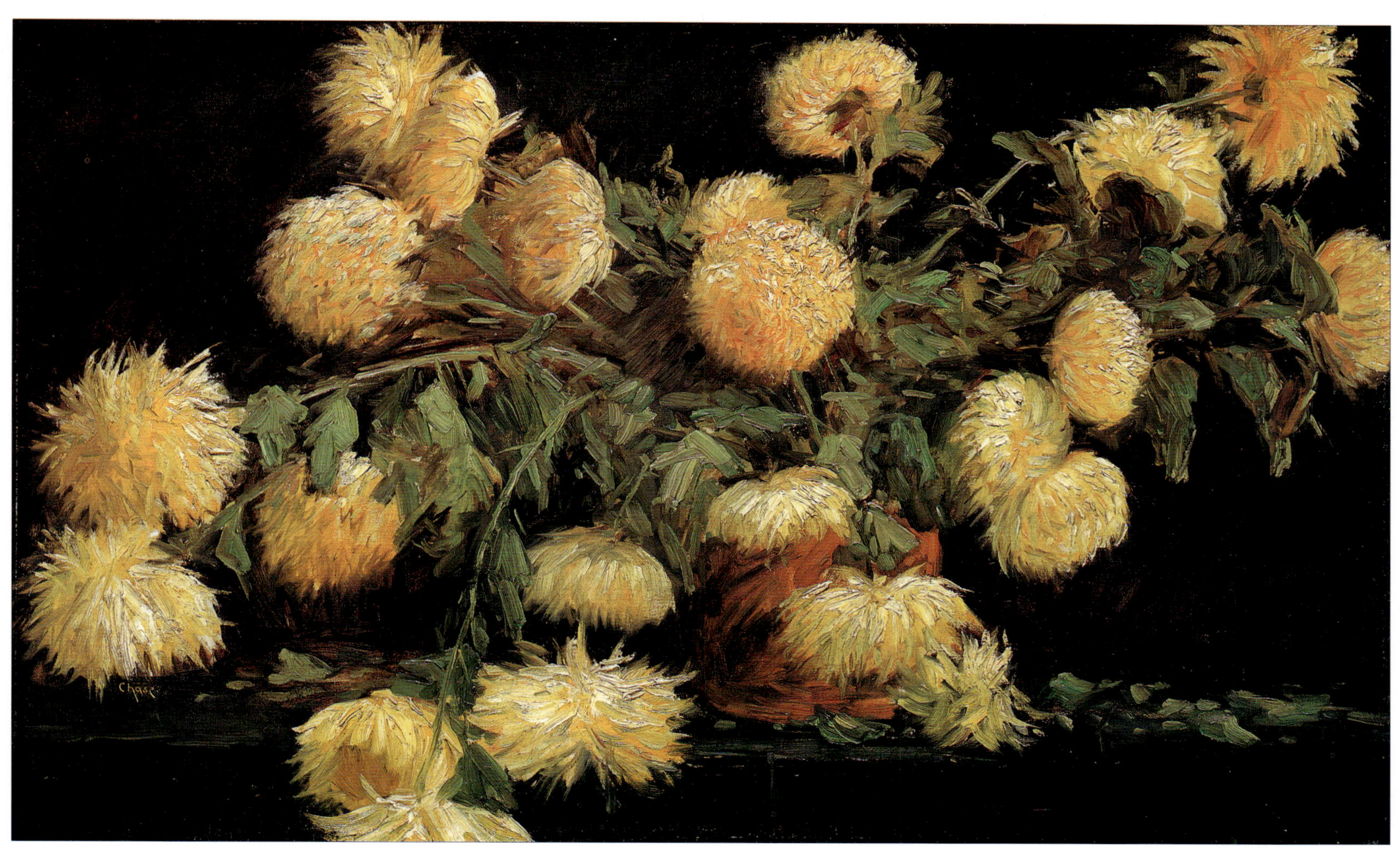
Chase

Martin Johnson Heade

Giant Magnolias

c. 1885–1895

Oil on canvas, 15¼" × 24" (38.7 × 61cm). The R.W. Norton Art Gallery, Shreveport, Louisiana.

In his early years, Martin Johnson Heade (1819–1904) was primarily a portraitist, working in almost photographic detail. He was later one of the Luminists, a group of painters who attempted to achieve the subtraction of the artist, creating a realism unblemished even by perceptible brush strokes. Heade also spent time in South America, drawing from life for a series of paintings of birds and flowers. The vividness of tropical blossoms is evident in this mesmerizing close-up of giant magnolias. Almost literally in the viewer's face, the flowers seem able to waft their seductive scent beyond the picture frame.

Unfortunately for the Luminists, Louis-Jacques-Mandé Daguerre had developed the first photographic process in 1839, and perhaps as a result, the modern public came to seek in painting something that the daguerreotype could not deliver. They wanted the touch and sensibility of the artist and the tangible matter of art, as well as its traditional representational effect. The Luminists' photographically realistic landscapes were thus out-of-date for the avant-garde collectors almost as soon as the paint dried.

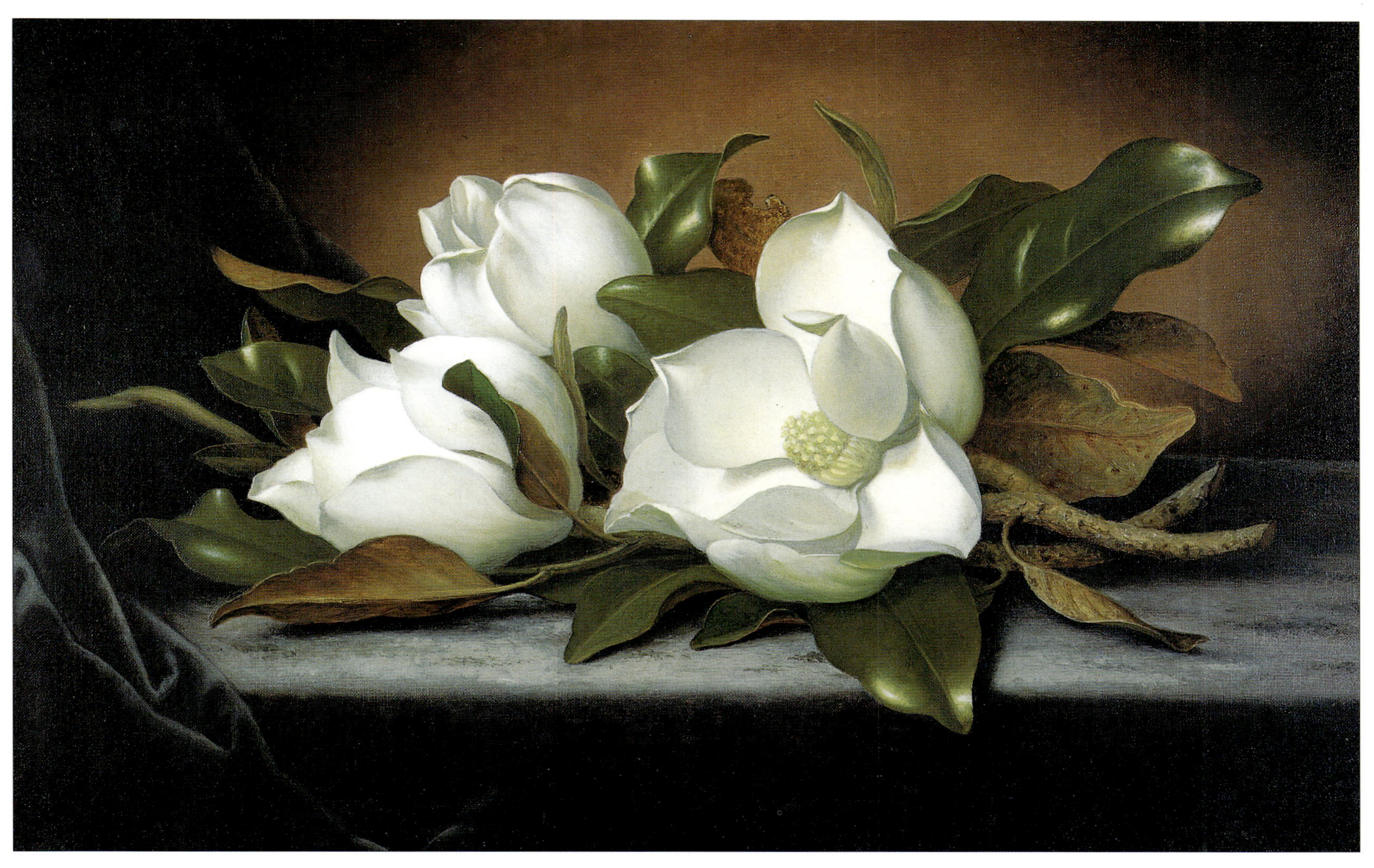

Vincent van Gogh

Imperial Crown Fritillaries in a Copper Vase

1886

Oil on canvas, 28½" × 23½" (72.3 × 59.6cm). Musée d'Orsay, Paris.

Vincent van Gogh (1853–1890) began painting in 1880, after an earlier, failed career as a minister in his native Holland. A subsequent stint as an art dealer brought him into contact with the Paris avant-garde, especially Paul Gauguin, with whom van Gogh shared rooms in Arles, in southern France. Vincent maintained his contact with the Paris art world through his brother, Theodore, who supported him both financially and emotionally, but who could not rescue his beloved sibling from mental illness. This work is wholly painterly—in echoing tones of color that are both studied and inspired, and in brushwork that illustrates van Gogh's awareness of the Pointillism that his fellow artists Georges-Pierre Seurat and Paul Signac were exploring. Van Gogh himself was to influence the later Expressionist and Symbolist painters. Yet despite the artist's discipline, the painting seems about to explode with urgent, vibrating energy, as if van Gogh were waging a personal battle to contain the living, overwhelming force of the universe in paint and brush strokes.

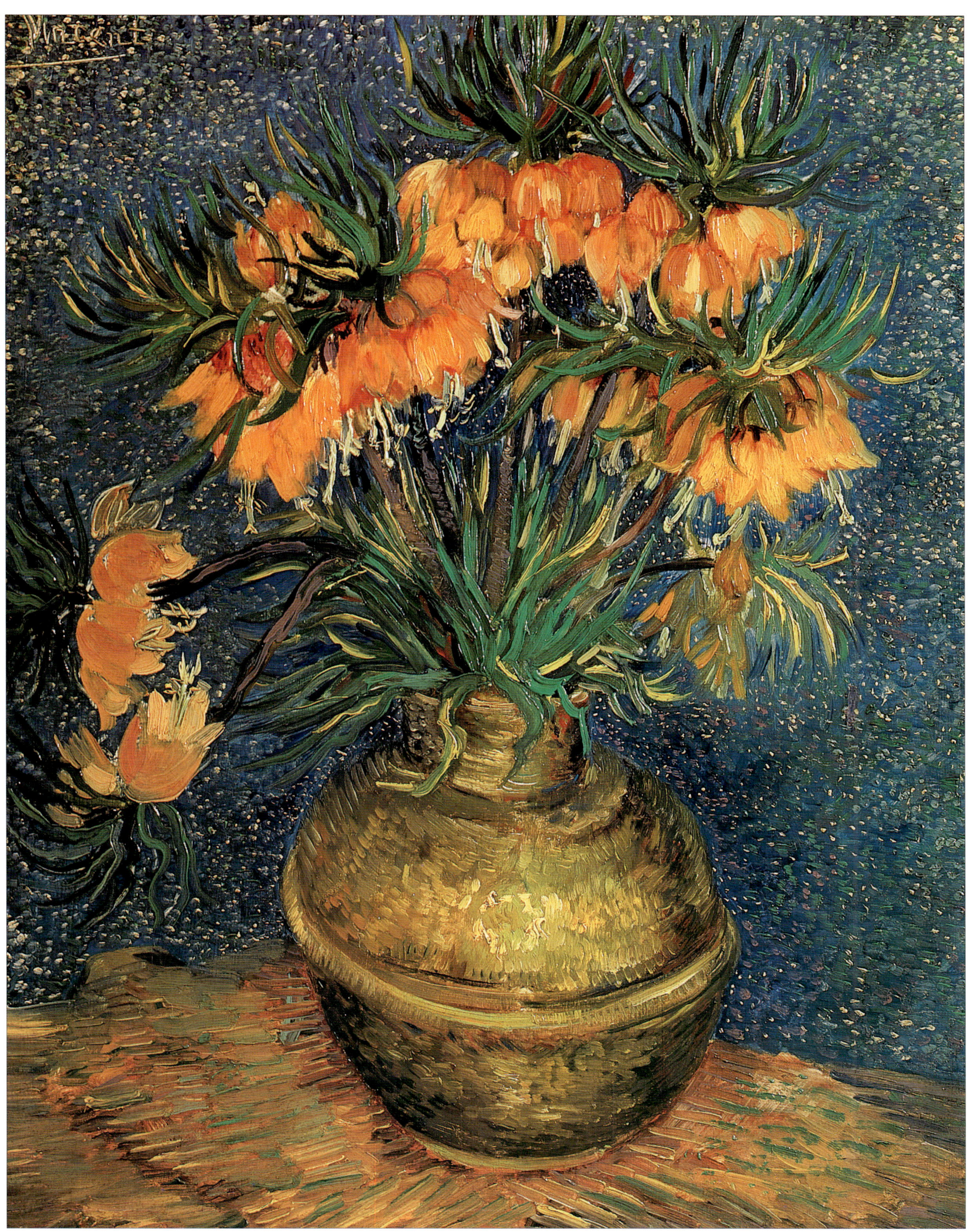

Félix Vallotton

Woman at the Piano (Madame Vallotton)

1904

Oil on canvas, 17" × 22½" (43.1 × 57.1cm). The Hermitage, Saint Petersburg.

There is something sweetly complete in this vignette of private life. We can almost smell the warm grasses and flowers from the garden outside the window and hear the musing piece the painter's wife plays. It is she who has picked the flowers that stand on the corner of the mantelpiece—where perhaps Félix Vallotton (1865–1925) had placed them to bring them within the frame of the picture—and the even humbler bouquet that sits atop the piano. She sits unself-consciously absorbed in her art, even as the painter records her with his own. Similar hues associate the wallpaper, the mantel, and the lady's informal day dress; this is a quiet tribute to the person who made the artist's home. There is much warmth, but no exaggerated house pride, to which the uneven edge of the clean but simple cloth on the table beneath the window testifies. The privateness of this scene is its subject. The most active force in it is the diagonal line between the standpoint of the viewer and the figure at the piano. This carefully worked-out painting suggests the feeling of entering a familiar room and experiencing at once a shock of happiness.

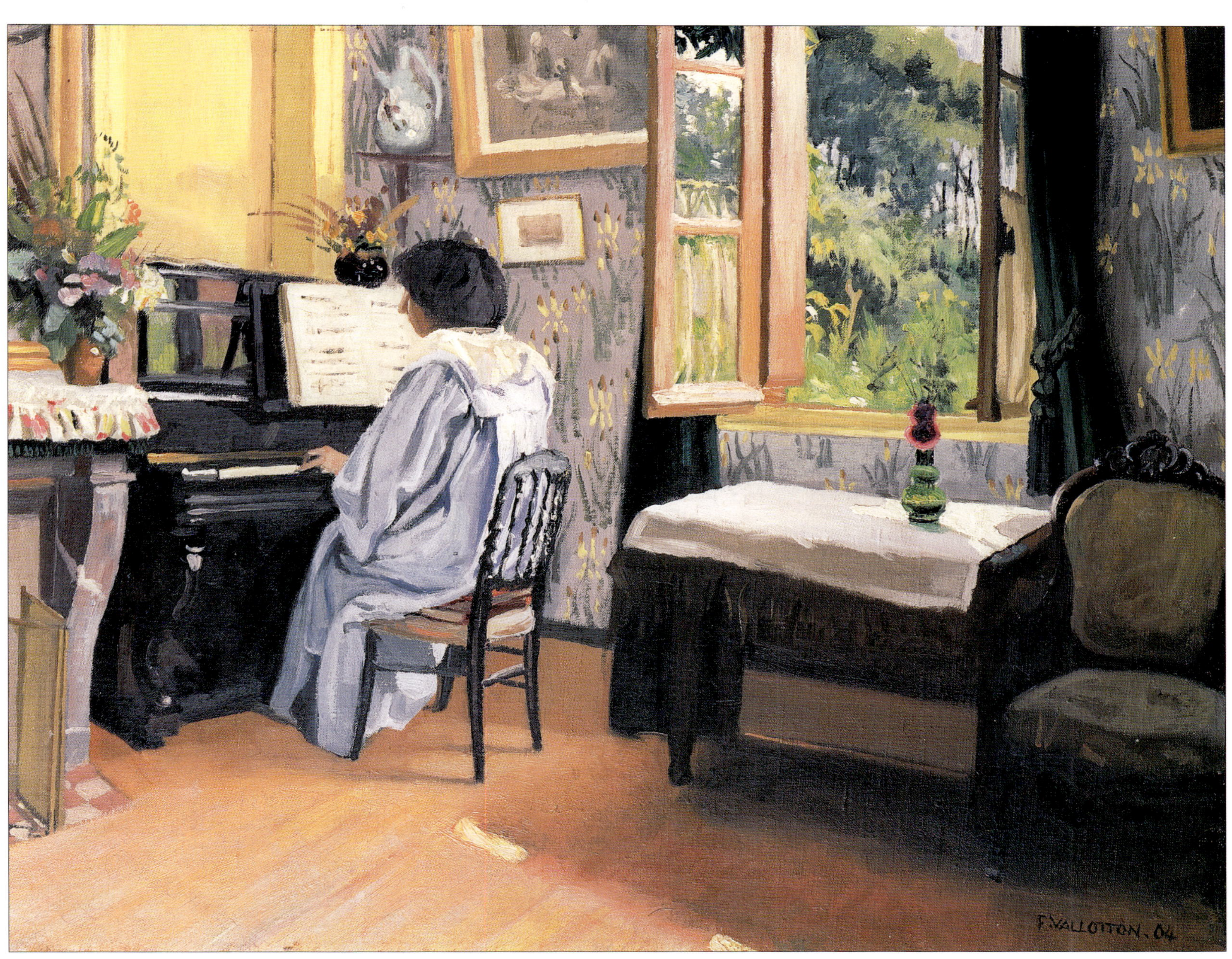
F. VALLOTTON. 04

Odilon Redon

Vase of Flowers

1914

Pastel on paper, 28¾" × 21⅛" (73 × 53.7cm). The Museum of Modern Art, New York City.

Odilon Redon (1840–1916) was a painter, lithographer, and engraver who worked in black and white for twenty years before bringing color into his art. Inspired by the grotesque symbolism of the writer Edgar Allan Poe and the painter Francisco Goya, Redon, in turn, was to influence the Surrealists. Given such interests, it might seem odd that Redon should choose a subject as pretty as flowers—but his interpretation holds true to his influences. Though these are recognizable flowers, picked by Madame Redon, they are presented with tunnel vision. They appear more realistic toward the center, then diffuse outward into metaphysical colors, surrounding the blossoms with a kind of aura that combines the colors of the flowers. The surface on which the vase stands is literally sketched in, while the vase itself is given its contours with the lightest of hands. The (relatively) realistic treatment of the container also points up the eventual strangeness of this most ordinary of still lifes.

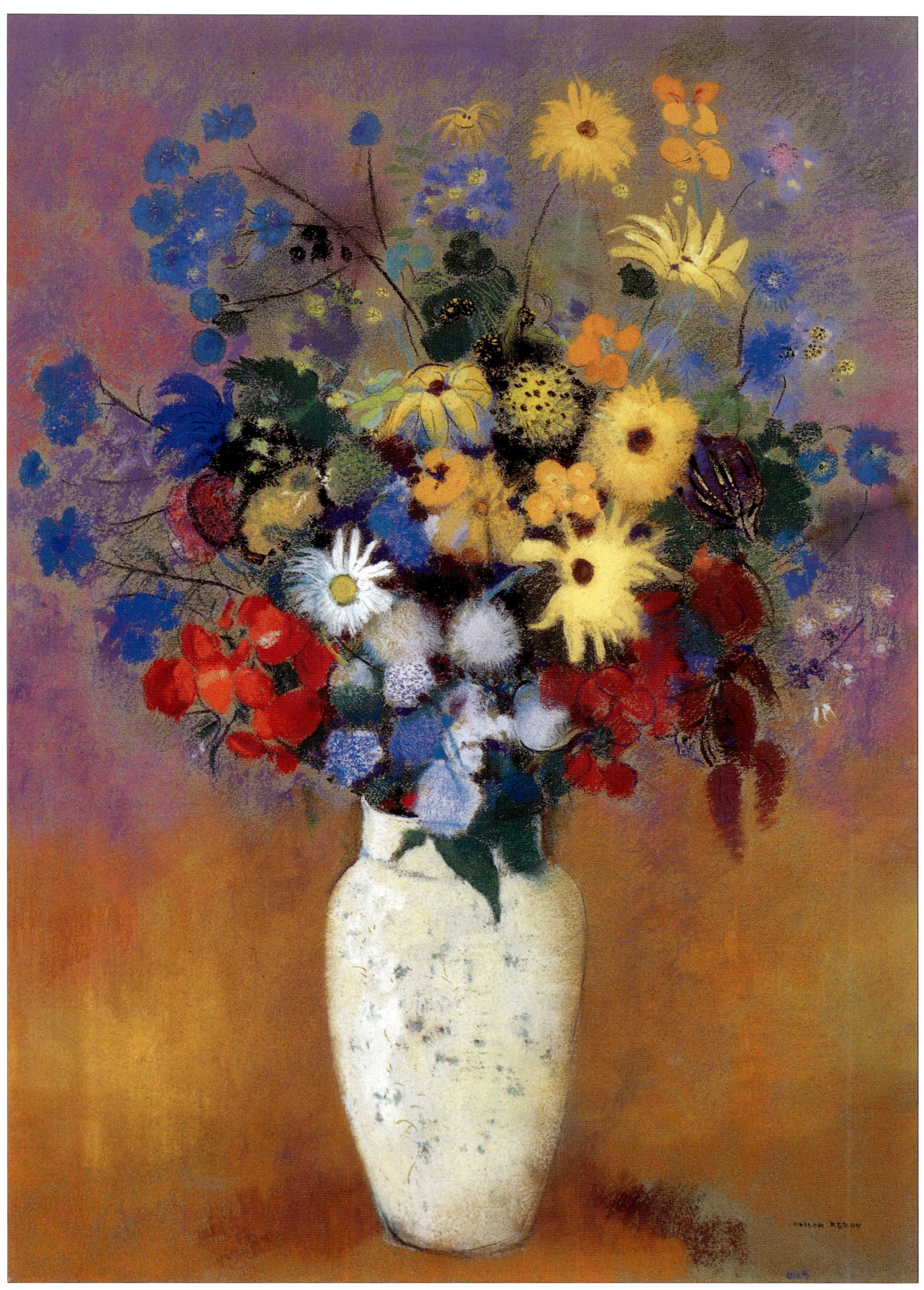

Henri Matisse

Anemones with Black Mirror

c. 1920

Oil on canvas, 26⅜" × 20⅗" (67 × 52.3cm).

Corporate Art Collection, The Reader's Digest Association, Inc., Pleasantville, New York.

As a young man, Henri Matisse (1869–1954) studied with Gustave Moreau, a leading Symbolist and later a painter of exotic, erotic works. Matisse, influenced early on by the Post-Impressionists, mastered a succession of styles, including Pointillism, which he abandoned, and Fauvism, of which he was a leading exponent. His works often include abstraction, as shown here in the blocks of color surrounding the mirror. Matisse painted this audaciously balanced composition during the winter when he was living in Nice, in the south of France. He was enamored of the light there, but one of the most striking aspects of this work is the absence of reflection precisely where a viewer might expect to find it. The mysterious and powerful black mirror recurs in several of Matisse's paintings; here, it looks almost oracular, like a fathomless pool in a goddess-ruled glade, over which hang the vivid and delicate blossoms. The anemone, in Greek myth, sprang from the blood of handsome, dying Adonis, who was cherished by both Aphrodite, goddess of love, and Persephone, queen of the underworld, but was killed by the jealous Ares, god of war. Matisse painted this work at a time when war was consuming Europe and the country's young men; in fact, the artist had attempted to enlist, but at forty-four was turned away as too old for the battlefield.

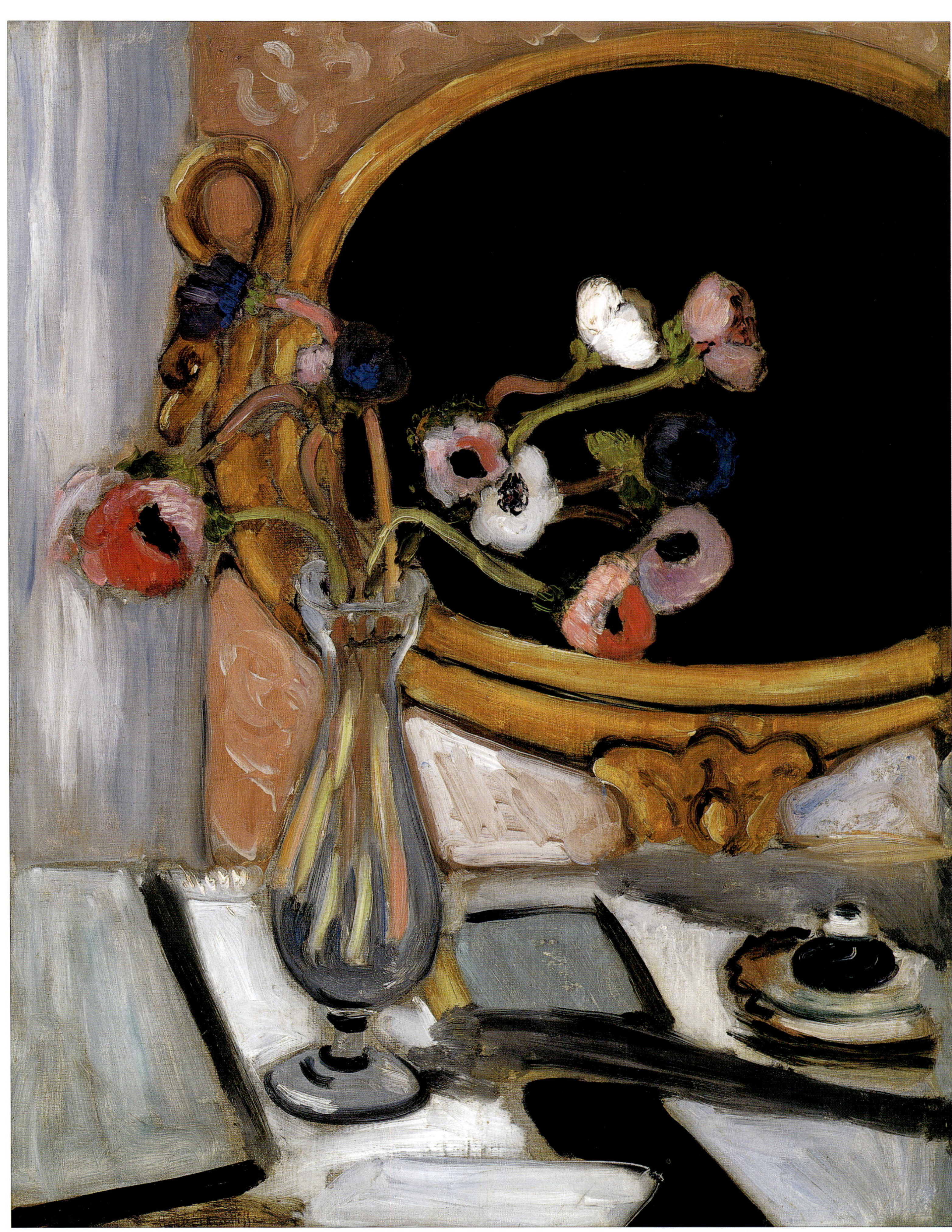

Romare Bearden

Interior

1939

Watercolor on paper, 14" × 22" (35.6 × 55.9cm).
The Carl Van Vechten Gallery of Fine Arts, Fisk University, Nashville.

Romare Bearden (1912–1988), whose mother ran the New York office of the African-American newspaper *Chicago Defender*, grew up amid the creative, collaborative ferment of the Harlem Renaissance. Beginning in about 1933, Bearden worked as an editorial cartoonist, perhaps inspired by his mother's journalism, and in 1936 he signed up for evening school at the New York Art Students League. Bearden took classes with, among others, the German-born George Grosz, whose sure, expressive lines and politically acerbic commentary intrigued Bearden, who studied the drawings of Honoré Daumier, Jean-Louis Forain, and Käthe Kollwitz. Grosz introduced Bearden to the artists Ingres, Dürer, Holbein, and Poussin, among others. *Interior*, which depicts a room only temporarily unoccupied, is a highly skilled, rather conventional work, recalling in particular Henri Matisse's early, colorful domesticity. As in Matisse's works, the flowers and other plants convey the uniqueness, freshness, and beauty of everyday life. In the 1940s, a few years after Bearden exhibited this watercolor at his first solo exhibition, he began to expand these concerns into the realm of social realism, peopling his interiors with African-Americans whose specific daily existence reflected humanity's universal experience.

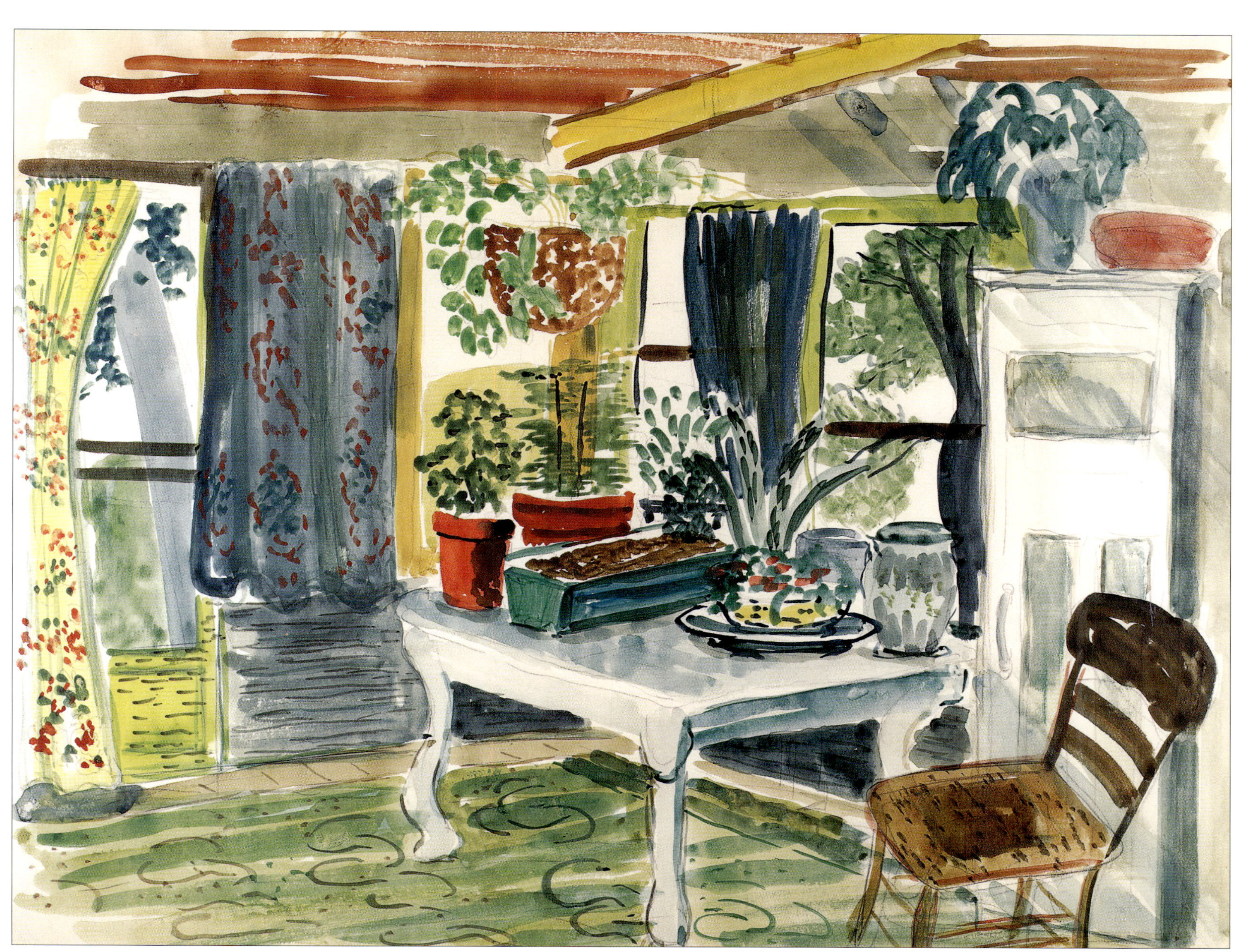

Horace Pippin

Victorian Parlor I

1945

Oil on canvas, 20" × 24" (50.8 × 61cm). The Metropolitan Museum of Art, New York City.

Painted in the same neoprimitive style as its surroundings, the outsize bouquet dominates this domestic interior by Horace Pippin (1888–1946), influencing our reading of the room and the relationship of its inhabitants. What is particularly Victorian, and slyly witty, is that the furniture is dressed, while the disconcertingly human-looking statues (in a parody of the Graeco-Roman artistic tradition) are not. The deep red plush curtains could keep the bright winter light out, but like the flowers inside, the nature outside the vast windows has pride of place and provides a visual breath of fresh air. Also Victorian is the clear distinction between the gentleman's chair and that of the lady. His is accompanied by pipe and open book; hers, by what may be a workbasket of the cotton she uses to crochet antimacassars, or wool for shawls. In Pippin's work, the bouquet does not separate the absent couple, but connects them, expressing the secret heart of this tidy but afffectionate home.

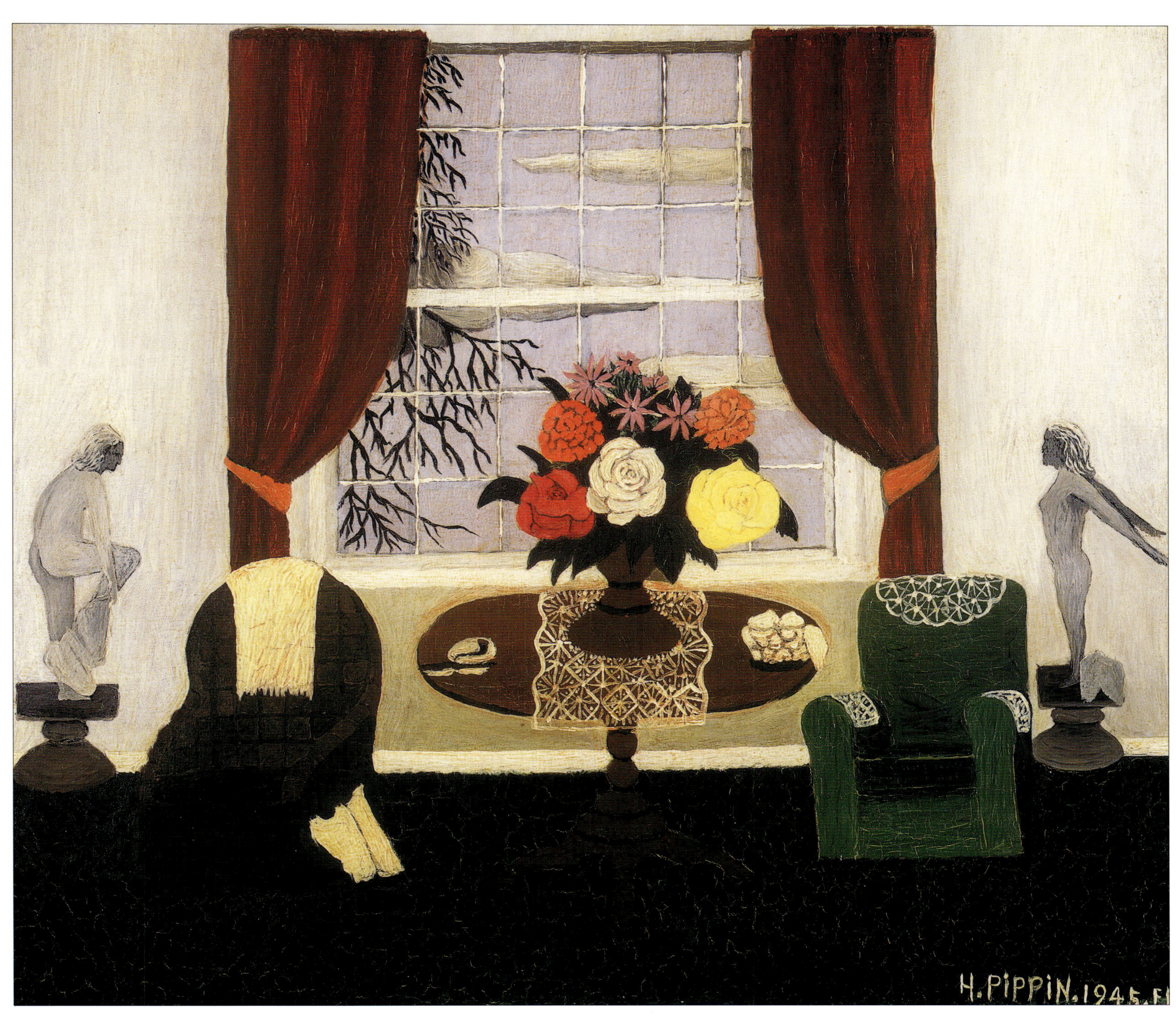
H.PIPPIN.1945.

Georgia O'Keeffe

Poppies

1950

Oil on canvas, 30" × 36" (76.2 × 91.4cm). Milwaukee Art Museum.

One of the most important American artists of the twentieth century, Georgia O'Keeffe (1887–1986), born near Sun Prairie, Wisconsin, was at the heart of photographer Alfred Stieglitz's circle in New York by 1907. In 1924, the same year she entered into a tempestuous marriage with Stieglitz, some twenty years her elder, O'Keeffe began working on abstract floral and other natural forms. In their tropically excessive size, O'Keeffe's flowers seem to transcend prettiness, even beauty, perhaps in order to magnify the sensuous physicality common to all things that live. However, reminding us that what we see in art is ours, just as the work will always belong intimately to the artist, O'Keeffe once stated flatly: "You write about my flower as if I think and see what you think and see of the flower and I don't." In 1929, O'Keeffe visited New Mexico, to which she eventually moved. Her later subject matter appears to be diametrically opposed to her earlier paintings, yet the sun-bleached animal skulls and sere desert landscapes are perhaps merely the reverse of the flowers—the husks that life leaves behind, the arid terrains where life, impossibly, survives.

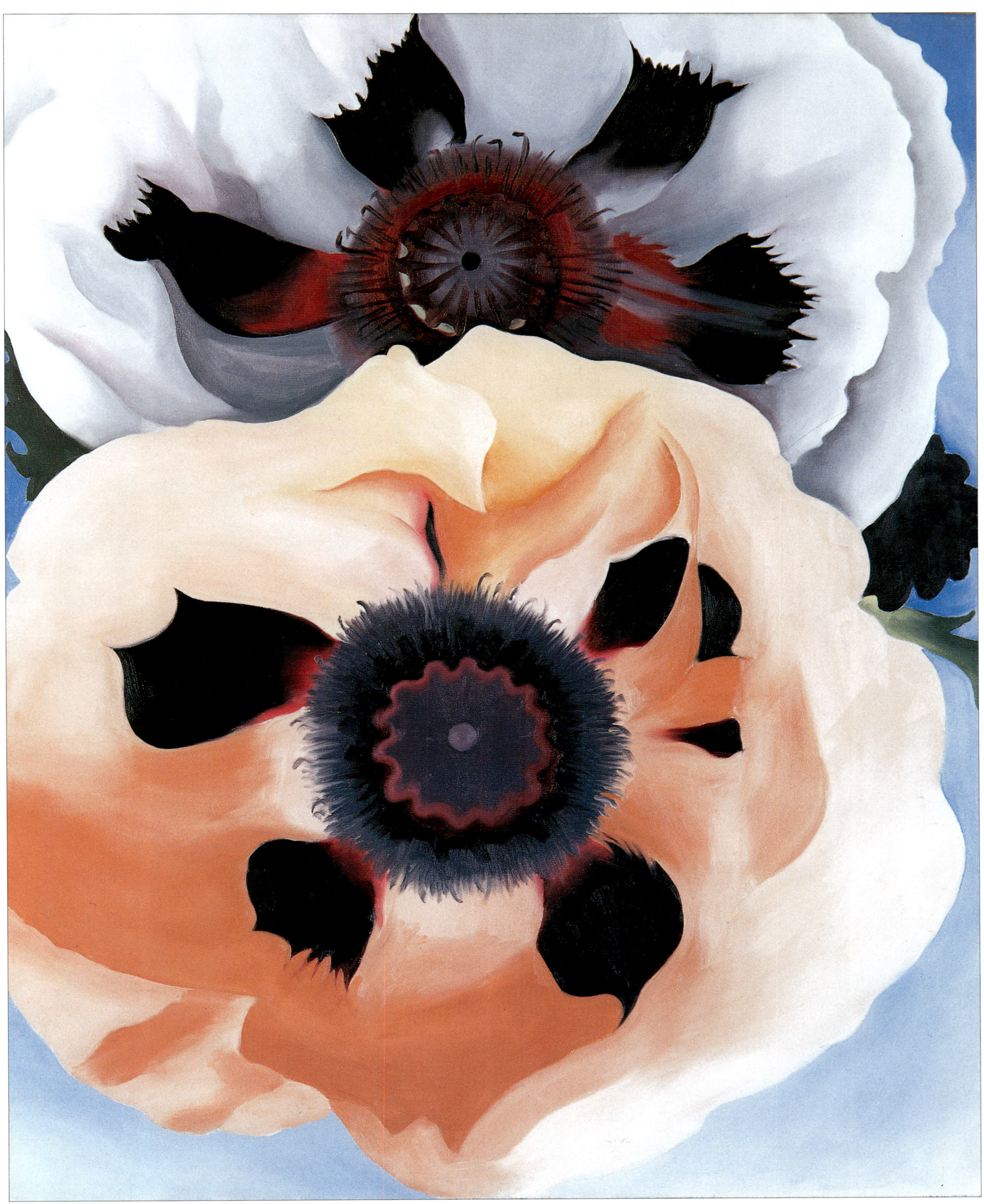

ELLIS WILSON

Funeral Procession

c. 1950

OIL ON MASONITE, 31½" × 32¾" (80 × 83.1CM).
AARON DOUGLAS COLLECTION, AMISTAD RESEARCH CENTER, TULANE UNIVERSITY, NEW ORLEANS.

Ellis Wilson (1899–1977) studied commercial art at the Art Institute of Chicago and pursued his studies during the Depression in New York City, where he was employed by the federally funded Works Progress Administration. There, along with other experimental young artists, he stretched the boundaries instilled by his academic training. Among his chief influences were Aaron Douglas and Horace Pippin, as well as El Greco, whose poetic elongation Wilson selectively applied. But it was the island of Haiti, with its long history and active artistic tradition, that kindled Wilson's visual and emotional imagination; much of Wilson's use of bright color derives from his time there and his work with Haitian artists. He first went to Haiti in the early 1950s, his visit the culmination of a search that began in the open markets of Charleston and passed through the Sea Islands off the Carolinas. In this work, the light-colored dresses among the somber hues recall the joy that exists alongside the sorrow of loss—the happiness expressed in certain congregations that a loved one has gone to God. In this procession, the mourners' dignity is accented by the grace notes of the bouquets they carry; death is balanced by the life carried within the pregnant woman in the center foreground.

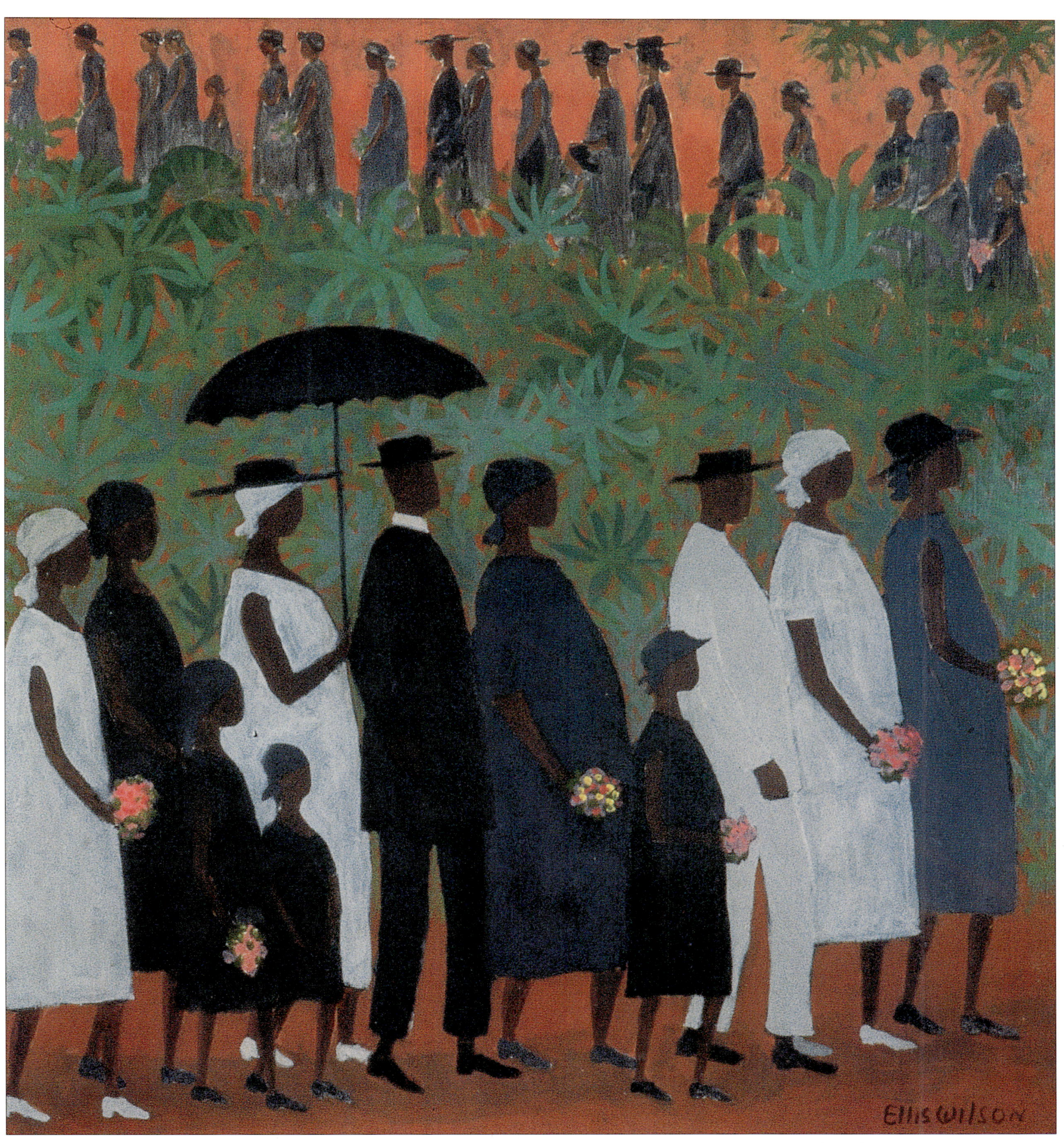
EllisWilson

David Hockney

Mount Fuji and Flowers

1972

Acrylic on canvas. 60" × 48" (152.4 × 121.9cm). The Metropolitan Museum of Art, New York City.

David Hockney (b. 1937) has a host of artistic identities, including painter, graphic designer, set designer, and photographer, and all these manifestations seem to come together to invite the viewer to participate in this work of art. The overall light appears flat, like the southern California sun so familiar to the expatriate, British-born Hockney. It is a light that washes out shadows and gradations, yet here it seems as clear as mountain air, an effect enhanced by Hockney's use of acrylic, a bright medium that looks as if it stays on the surface of the canvas. The viewer's eye travels between the three bright areas, from the peak of the timeless, limitless sacred mountain down to each of the specific and ephemeral blossoms, and back again. The surface and the sill at the bottom of the picture imply a viewer, whose mind and heart determine what is perceived. In the title, the alliteration of the words *Fuji* and *Flowers* brings in a literary aspect. The result might be a kind of haiku—an unrhymed Japanese poem of three lines—that each viewer creates by connecting the elements of the painting with personal experience and feeling.

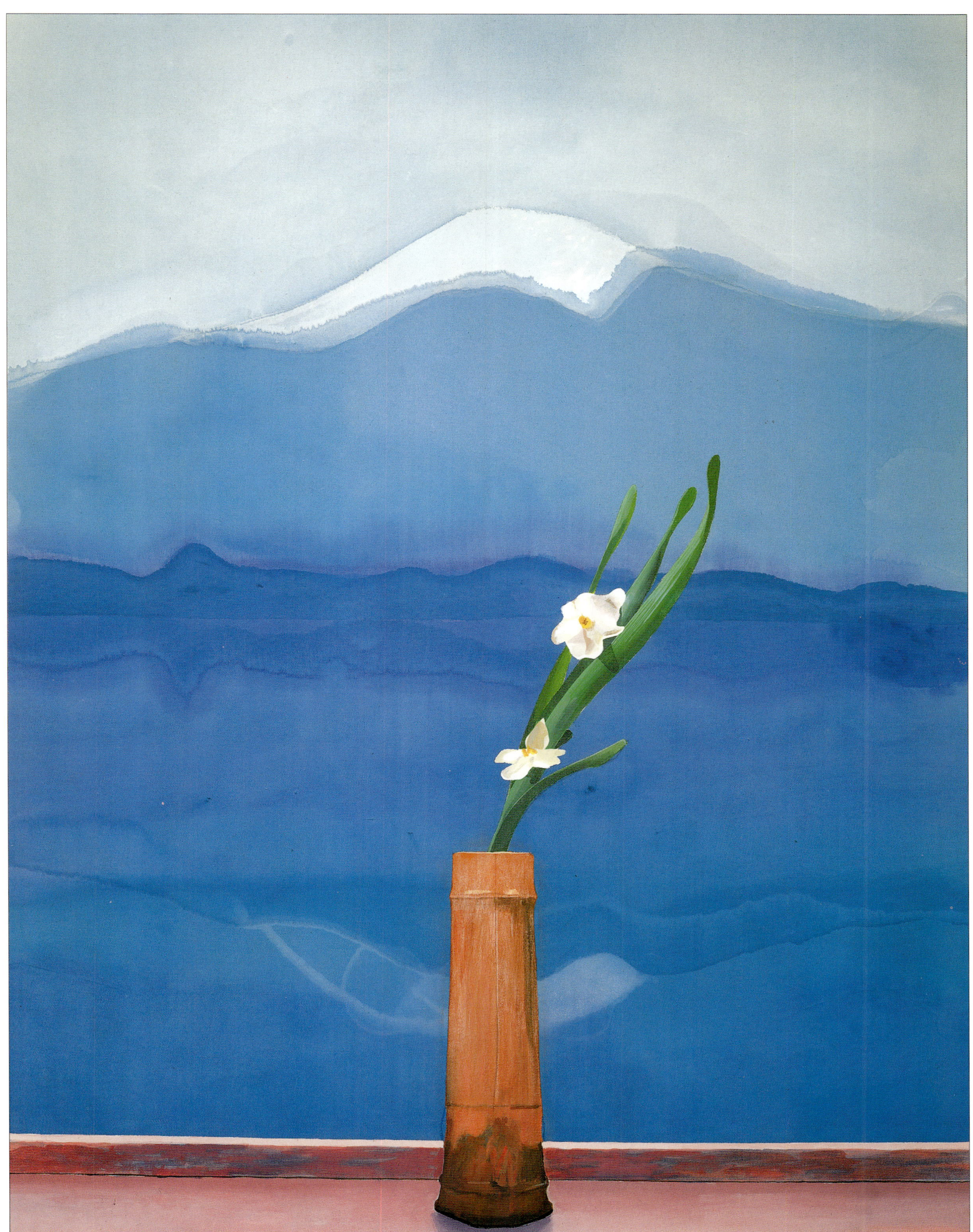

Mary Frank

Untitled

1977

Monotype on two sheets, printed in color. 35½" × 23 13/16" (90.2 × 60.4cm).
The Museum of Modern Art, New York City.

The dancing figure in the lower right-hand corner reminds the viewer that the British-born Mary Frank (b. 1933) was herself a dancer for four years with the rigorous American master Martha Graham before studying for a time with the New York painters Max Beckmann and Hans Hofmann. While Beckmann is known for social commentary and violent images, Hofmann was a founding Abstract Expressionist who experimented with form and improvisation. Frank has principally worked as a sculptor—perhaps her dance training has extended to an awareness of objects in space—but also as a painter and printmaker. This monotype, or single print, downplays the intense color that is the most obvious characteristic of an amaryllis, yet seems otherwise to display the kind of botanical detail traditional for centuries in the depiction of flowers. There are the flowers, buds, stems, and top of the bulb, but the textured gray on the plate adds ambiguity, as do the organic shapes that suggest connections between the human and vegetable realms. Then there is that fleeing, elfin creature....

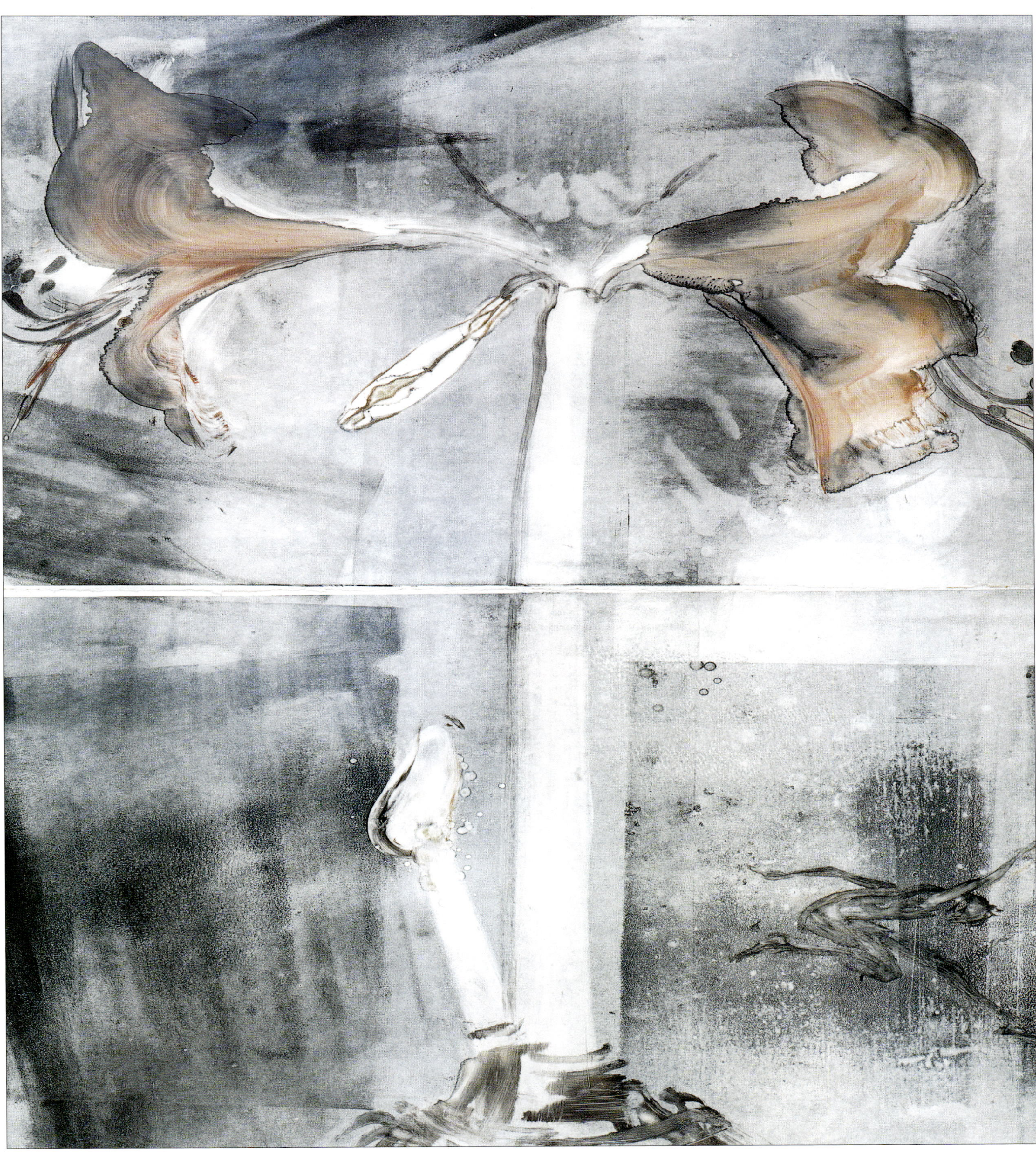

Photography Credits

Vincent van Gogh, *Irises*, oil on canvas, 29" × 36¼" (73.7 × 93.1cm), The Metropolitan Museum of Art, gift of Adele R. Levy, 1958, photograph by Malcolm Varon (58.187)

Jan Brueghel the Elder, *Bouquet of Flowers*, c. 1619–1620, oil on oak panel, 25¼" × 23¼" (64.1 × 59cm), Preussiches Kulterbesitz, Nationalgalerie, Staatliche Museen zu Berlin

Édouard Manet, *Two Roses on a Tablecloth*, 1882–1883, oil on canvas, 7⅝" × 9½" (19.3 × 24.2cm), The Museum of Modern Art, New York, William S. Paley Collection, photograph © 1996 The Museum of Modern Art, New York

Henri Fantin-Latour, *Bouquet of Roses and Nasturtiums in a Vase*, 1883, oil on canvas, 11" × 14" (28 × 36cm), The Hermitage, Saint Petersburg

Unknown, Deir el Bahri, Thebes, Egyptian, *Funerary Papyrus*, third intermediate period, Twenty-first Dynasty, c. 1039–991 B.C., 13¾"–14⅛" (34.9–35.8cm) in height, excavations of The Metropolitan Museum of Art, 1929, Rogers Fund, 1930 (30.3.31)

Unknown, *Tughra of Süleyman the Magnificent*, 16th century, ink, colors, and gold on paper, 20½" × 25⅜", (52.1 × 64.5cm), The Metropolitan Museum of Art, Rogers Fund, 1938 (38.149.1)

Sofonisba Anguisciola, *A Young Lady in Profile*, late 16th century, oil on canvas, 27" × 20½" (68.5 × 52cm), The Hermitage, Saint Petersburg

Ambrosius Bosschaert the Elder, *Large Bouquet in a Wan-Li Vase on Gun Metal Base*, oil on mahogany panel, 19¹³⁄₁₆" × 14" (50.3 × 35.5cm), Kunsthistorisches Museum, Vienna

Jacob Jordaens, *Madonna and Child Wreathed with Flowers*, c. 1618, oil on canvas, 41" × 29" (104.1 × 73.6cm), The Hermitage, Saint Petersburg

Rembrandt, *Lady with a Pink*, mid- to late 17th century, oil on canvas, 36¼" × 29⅜" (92.1 × 74.6cm), The Metropolitan Museum of Art, Bequest of Benjamin Altman, 1913 (14.40.622)

Jean-Baptiste Monnoyer, *Flowers and Fruit*, mid- to late 17th century, oil on canvas, 29" × 48" (73.6 × 121.9cm), The Hermitage, Saint Petersburg

Elisabetta Sirani, *Virgin and Child*, 1663, oil on canvas, 34" × 27½" (86.3 × 69.8cm), The National Museum of Women in the Arts, Washington, D.C., Gift of Wallace and Wilhelmina Holladay

Shih-t'ao, *Peonies*, c. 1698, ink and color on paper, The Arthur M. Sackler Collection, New York

Rachel Ruysch, *Roses, Convolvulus, Poppies and Other Flowers in an Urn on a Stone Ledge*, c.1745, oil on canvas, 42½" × 33" (108 × 83.8cm), The National Museum of Women in the Arts, Washington, D.C., Gift of Wallace and Wilhelmina Holladay

Marie-Louise Élisabeth Vigée-Lebrun, *Marie-Antoinette*, 1783, oil on canvas, 45" × 35" (113 × 87cm), Château de Versailles, France, © Photo RMN

Ann Walgrave Warner, *Coverlet*, c. 1800, linen and cotton, 104" × 90" (264.2 × 228.6cm), The Metropolitan Museum of Art, Gift of Catherine E. Cotheal, 1938 (38.59), photograph by John Bigelow Taylor

John La Farge, *Magnolia*, c. 1863, oil on panel, 16" × 11¼" (40.6 × 28.5cm), The Berkshire Museum (1956.15.2)

Édouard Manet, *Peonies*, 1864, oil on canvas, 23⅜" × 13⅞" (59.4 × 35.2cm), The Metropolitan Museum of Art, bequest of Joan Whitney Payson, 1975 (1976.201.16)

Edgar Degas, *Woman with Chrysanthemums*, 1865, oil on canvas, 29" × 36½" (73.7 × 92.7cm), The Metropolitan Museum of Art, bequest of Mrs. H.O. Havemeyer, 1929, The H.O. Havemeyer Collection (29.100.128)

Hans Thoma, *Bouquet of Wild Flowers*, 1872, oil on canvas, 29½" × 21⅝" (75 × 55cm), Preussiches Kulturbesitz, Nationalgalerie, Staatliche Museen zu Berlin

Paul Cézanne, *Bouquet of Flowers in a Vase*, 1873–1875, oil on canvas, 22" × 18" (56 × 46cm), The Hermitage, Saint Petersburg

Berthe Morisot, *Lady at Her Toilet*, c. 1875, oil on canvas, 23¾" × 31½" (60.3 × 80.4cm), Stickney Fund, 1924.127, © 1991 The Art Institute of Chicago, All Rights Reserved

Unknown, *Chrysanthemums*, fourth quarter 19th century, oil on canvas, 26⅞" × 44¾" (68.2 × 113.7cm), National Gallery of Art, Washington, D.C., Chester Dale Collection

Martin Johnson Heade, *Giant Magnolias*, c.1885–1895, oil on canvas, 15¼" × 24" (38.7 × 61cm), The R.W. Norton Art Gallery, Shreveport, Louisiana

Vincent van Gogh, *Imperial Crown Fritillaries in a Copper Vase*, 1886, oil on canvas, 28½" × 23½" (72.3 × 59.6cm), Musée d'Orsay, Paris, Erich Lessing/Art Resource, NY

Félix Vallotton, *Woman at the Piano (Madame Vallotton)*, 1904, oil on canvas, 17" × 22½" (43.1 × 57.1cm), The Hermitage, Saint Petersburg

Odilon Redon, *Vase of Flowers*, 1914, pastel on paper, 28¾" × 21⅛" (73 × 53.7cm), The Museum of Modern Art, New York, William S. Paley Collection, photograph © 1996 The Museum of Modern Art, New York

Henri Matisse, *Anemones with Black Mirror*, c. 1920, oil on canvas, 26⅜" × 20⅗" (67 × 52.3cm), Corporate Art Collection, The Reader's Digest Association, Inc.

Romare Bearden, *Interior*, 1939, watercolor on paper, 14" × 22" (35.6 × 55.9cm), The Carl Van Vechten Gallery of Fine Arts, Fisk University, Nashville, TN

Horace Pippin, *Victorian Parlor I*, 1945, oil on canvas, 20" × 24" (50.8 × 61cm), The Metropolitan Museum of Art, bequest of Jane Kendall Gingrich, 1982 (1982.55.5)

Georgia O'Keeffe, *Poppies*, 1950, oil on canvas, 36" × 30" (76.2 × 91.4cm), Milwaukee Art Museum, Gift of Mrs. Harry Lynde Bradley

Ellis Wilson, *Funeral Procession*, c. 1950, oil on masonite, 31½" × 32¾" (80 × 83.1cm), Aaron Douglas Collection, Amistad Research Center, Tulane University, New Orleans

David Hockney, *Mount Fuji and Flowers*, 1972, acrylic on canvas, 60" × 48" (152.4 × 121.9cm), The Metropolitan Museum of Art, purchase, Mrs. Arthur Hays Sulzberger Gift, 1972 (1972.128), photograph by Lynton Gardiner

Mary Frank, *Untitled*, 1977, monotype on two sheets, printed in color, 35½" × 23¹³⁄₁₆" (90.2 × 60.4cm), The Museum of Modern Art, New York, Mrs. E.B. Parkinson Fund, photograph © 1996 The Museum of Modern Art, New York

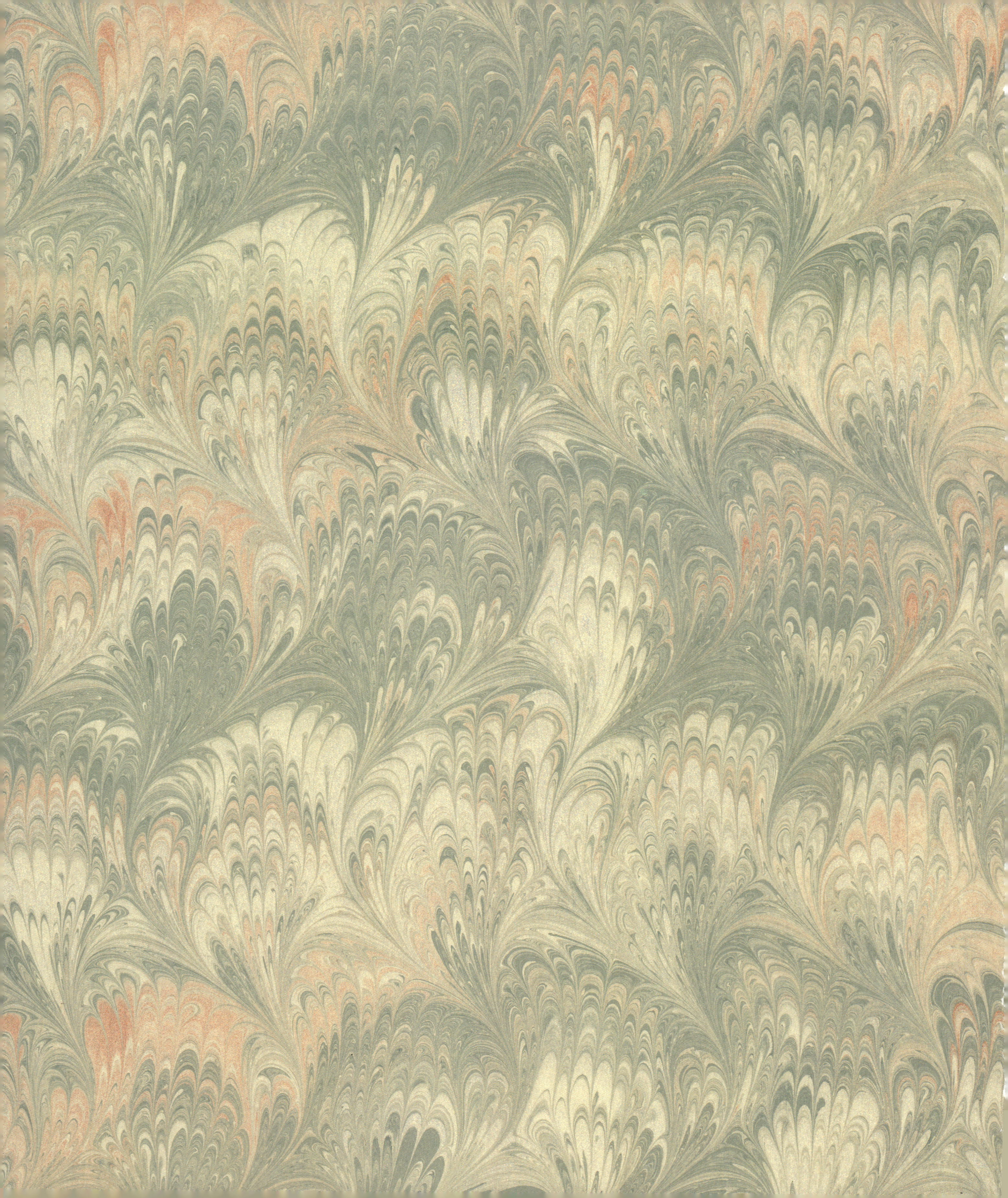